Care Standards Act 2000

CHAPTER 14

ARRANGEMENT OF SECTIONS

PART I

INTRODUCTORY

Preliminary

Section
1. Children's homes.
2. Independent hospitals etc.
3. Care homes.
4. Other basic definitions.

Registration authorities

5. Registration authorities.
6. National Care Standards Commission.
7. General duties of the Commission.
8. General functions of the Assembly.
9. Co-operative working.
10. Inquiries.

PART II

ESTABLISHMENTS AND AGENCIES

Registration

11. Requirement to register.
12. Applications for registration.
13. Grant or refusal of registration.
14. Cancellation of registration.
15. Applications by registered persons.
16. Regulations about registration.

Registration procedure

17. Notice of proposals.
18. Right to make representations.
19. Notice of decisions.
20. Urgent procedure for cancellation etc.
21. Appeals to the Tribunal.

Regulations and standards

Section
22. Regulation of establishments and agencies.
23. National minimum standards.

Offences

24. Failure to comply with conditions.
25. Contravention of regulations.
26. False descriptions of establishments and agencies.
27. False statements in applications.
28. Failure to display certificate of registration.
29. Proceedings for offences.
30. Offences by bodies corporate.

Miscellaneous and supplemental

31. Inspections by persons authorised by registration authority.
32. Inspections: supplementary.
33. Annual returns.
34. Liquidators etc.
35. Death of registered person.
36. Provision of copies of registers.
37. Service of documents.
38. Transfers of staff under Part II.
39. Temporary extension of meaning of "nursing home".
40. Temporary extension of meaning of "children's home".
41. Children's homes: temporary provision about cancellation of registration.
42. Power to extend the application of Part II.

PART III

LOCAL AUTHORITY SERVICES

43. Introductory.
44. General powers of the Commission.
45. Inspection by registration authority of adoption and fostering services.
46. Inspections: supplementary.
47. Action following inspection.
48. Regulation of the exercise of relevant fostering functions.
49. National minimum standards.
50. Annual returns.
51. Annual fee.
52. Contravention of regulations.
53. Offences: general provisions.

PART IV

SOCIAL CARE WORKERS

Preliminary

54. Care Councils.
55. Interpretation.

Registration

56. The register.

Section
57. Applications for registration.
58. Grant or refusal of registration.
59. Removal etc. from register.
60. Rules about registration.
61. Use of title "social worker" etc.

Codes of practice

62. Codes of practice.

Training

63. Approval of courses etc.
64. Qualifications gained outside a Council's area.
65. Post registration training.
66. Visitors for certain social work courses.
67. Functions of the appropriate Minister.

Miscellaneous and supplemental

68. Appeals to the Tribunal.
69. Publication etc. of register.
70. Abolition of Central Council for Education and Training in Social Work.
71. Rules.

PART V

THE CHILDREN'S COMMISSIONER FOR WALES

72. Children's Commissioner for Wales.
73. Review and monitoring of arrangements.
74. Examination of cases.
75. Obstruction etc.
76. Further functions.
77. Restrictions.
78. Interpretation.

PART VI

CHILD MINDING AND DAY CARE

79. Amendment of Children Act 1989.

PART VII

PROTECTION OF CHILDREN AND VULNERABLE ADULTS

Protection of vulnerable adults

80. Basic definitions.
81. Duty of Secretary of State to keep list.
82. Persons who provide care for vulnerable adults: duty to refer.
83. Employment agencies and businesses: duty to refer.
84. Power of registration authority to refer.
85. Individuals named in the findings of certain inquiries.
86. Appeals against inclusion in list.
87. Applications for removal from list.
88. Conditions for application under section 87.
89. Effect of inclusion in list.

Section

90. Searches of list under Part V of Police Act 1997.
91. Access to list before commencement of section 90.
92. Persons referred for inclusion in list under Protection of Children Act 1999.
93. Power to extend Part VII.

The list kept under section 1 of the 1999 Act

94. Employment agencies and businesses.
95. Inclusion in 1999 Act list on reference by certain authorities.
96. Inclusion in 1999 Act list of individuals named in findings of certain inquiries.
97. Inclusion in 1999 Act list on reference under this Part.
98. Individuals providing care funded by direct payments.
99. Transfer from Consultancy Service Index of individuals named in past inquiries.

Restrictions on working with children in independent schools

100. Additional ground of complaint.
101. Effect of inclusion in 1996 Act list.
102. Searches of 1996 Act list.

General

103. Temporary provision for access to lists.
104. Suitability to adopt a child: searches of lists.

PART VIII

MISCELLANEOUS

Boarding schools and colleges

105. Welfare of children in boarding schools and colleges.
106. Suspension of duty under section 87(3) of the 1989 Act.
107. Boarding schools: national minimum standards.
108. Annual fee for boarding school inspections.
109. Inspection of schools etc. by persons authorised by Secretary of State.

Fostering

110. Extension of Part IX to school children during holidays.

Employment agencies

111. Nurses Agencies.

Charges for local authority welfare services

112. Charges for local authority welfare services.

Part IX

General and supplemental

Chapter I

General

Section
113. Default powers of appropriate Minister.
114. Schemes for the transfer of staff.
115. Effect of schemes.
116. Minor and consequential amendments.
117. Transitional provisions, savings and repeals.

Chapter II

Supplemental

118. Orders and regulations.
119. Supplementary and consequential provision etc.
120. Wales.
121. General interpretation etc.
122. Commencement.
123. Short title and extent.

Schedules:

    Schedule 1—The Commission and the Councils.
    Schedule 2—The Children's Commissioner for Wales.
    Schedule 3—Child minding and day care for young children.
    Schedule 4—Minor and consequential amendments.
    Schedule 5—Transitional provisions and savings.
    Schedule 6—Repeals.

Care Standards Act 2000

2000 CHAPTER 14

An Act to establish a National Care Standards Commission; to make provision for the registration and regulation of children's homes, independent hospitals, independent clinics, care homes, residential family centres, independent medical agencies, domiciliary care agencies, fostering agencies, nurses agencies and voluntary adoption agencies; to make provision for the regulation and inspection of local authority fostering and adoption services; to establish a General Social Care Council and a Care Council for Wales and make provision for the registration, regulation and training of social care workers; to establish a Children's Commissioner for Wales; to make provision for the registration, regulation and training of those providing child minding or day care; to make provision for the protection of children and vulnerable adults; to amend the law about children looked after in schools and colleges; to repeal the Nurses Agencies Act 1957; to amend Schedule 1 to the Local Authority Social Services Act 1970; and for connected purposes.

[20th July 2000]

BE IT ENACTED by the Queen's most Excellent Majesty, by and with the advice and consent of the Lords Spiritual and Temporal, and Commons, in this present Parliament assembled, and by the authority of the same, as follows:—

PART I

INTRODUCTORY

Preliminary

1.—(1) Subsections (2) to (6) have effect for the purposes of this Act. Children's homes.

(2) An establishment is a children's home (subject to the following provisions of this section) if it provides care and accommodation wholly or mainly for children.

(3) An establishment is not a children's home merely because a child is cared for and accommodated there by a parent or relative of his or by a foster parent.

(4) An establishment is not a children's home if it is—

(a) a health service hospital;

(b) an independent hospital or an independent clinic; or

(c) a residential family centre,

or if it is of a description excepted by regulations.

(5) Subject to subsection (6), an establishment is not a children's home if it is a school.

(6) A school is a children's home at any time if at that time accommodation is provided for children at the school and either—

(a) in each year that fell within the period of two years ending at that time, accommodation was provided for children, either at the school or under arrangements made by the proprietor of the school, for more than 295 days; or

(b) it is intended to provide accommodation for children, either at the school or under arrangements made by the proprietor of the school, for more than 295 days in any year;

and in this subsection "year" means a period of twelve months.

But accommodation shall not for the purposes of paragraph (a) be regarded as provided to children for a number of days unless there is at least one child to whom it is provided for that number of days; and paragraph (b) shall be construed accordingly.

(7) For the purposes of this section a person is a foster parent in relation to a child if—

(a) he is a local authority foster parent in relation to the child;

(b) he is a foster parent with whom a child has been placed by a voluntary organisation under section 59(1)(a) of the 1989 Act; or

(c) he fosters the child privately.

Independent hospitals etc.

2.—(1) Subsections (2) to (6) apply for the purposes of this Act.

(2) A hospital which is not a health service hospital is an independent hospital.

(3) "Hospital" (except in the expression health service hospital) means—

(a) an establishment—

(i) the main purpose of which is to provide medical or psychiatric treatment for illness or mental disorder or palliative care; or

(ii) in which (whether or not other services are also provided) any of the listed services are provided;

(b) any other establishment in which treatment or nursing (or both) are provided for persons liable to be detained under the Mental Health Act 1983.

1983 c. 20.

(4) "Independent clinic" means an establishment of a prescribed kind (not being a hospital) in which services are provided by medical practitioners (whether or not any services are also provided for the purposes of the establishment elsewhere).

But an establishment in which, or for the purposes of which, services are provided by medical practitioners in pursuance of the National Health Service Act 1977 is not an independent clinic.

1977 c. 49.

(5) "Independent medical agency" means an undertaking (not being an independent clinic) which consists of or includes the provision of services by medical practitioners.

But if any of the services are provided for the purposes of an independent clinic, or by medical practitioners in pursuance of the National Health Service Act 1977, it is not an independent medical agency.

(6) References to a person liable to be detained under the Mental Health Act 1983 do not include a person absent in pursuance of leave granted under section 17 of that Act.

1983 c. 20.

(7) In this section "listed services" means—

(a) medical treatment under anaesthesia or sedation;

(b) dental treatment under general anaesthesia;

(c) obstetric services and, in connection with childbirth, medical services;

(d) termination of pregnancies;

(e) cosmetic surgery;

(f) treatment using prescribed techniques or prescribed technology.

(8) Regulations may—

(a) except any description of establishment from the definitions in subsections (2) to (4);

(b) except any description of undertaking from the definition in subsection (5);

(c) modify the definition in subsection (7).

3.—(1) For the purposes of this Act, an establishment is a care home if it provides accommodation, together with nursing or personal care, for any of the following persons.

Care homes.

(2) They are—

(a) persons who are or have been ill;

(b) persons who have or have had a mental disorder;

(c) persons who are disabled or infirm;

(d) persons who are or have been dependent on alcohol or drugs.

(3) But an establishment is not a care home if it is—

(a) a hospital;

(b) an independent clinic; or

(c) a children's home,

or if it is of a description excepted by regulations.

4.—(1) This section has effect for the purposes of this Act.

(2) "Residential family centre" means, subject to subsection (6), any establishment at which—

(a) accommodation is provided for children and their parents;

(b) the parents' capacity to respond to the children's needs and to safeguard their welfare is monitored or assessed; and

(c) the parents are given such advice, guidance or counselling as is considered necessary.

In this subsection "parent", in relation to a child, includes any person who is looking after him.

(3) "Domiciliary care agency" means, subject to subsection (6), an undertaking which consists of or includes arranging the provision of personal care in their own homes for persons who by reason of illness, infirmity or disability are unable to provide it for themselves without assistance.

(4) "Fostering agency" means, subject to subsection (6)—

(a) an undertaking which consists of or includes discharging functions of local authorities in connection with the placing of children with foster parents; or

(b) a voluntary organisation which places children with foster parents under section 59(1) of the 1989 Act.

(5) "Nurses agency" means, subject to subsection (6), an employment agency or employment business, being (in either case) a business which consists of or includes supplying, or providing services for the purpose of supplying, registered nurses, registered midwives or registered health visitors.

(6) The definitions in subsections (2) to (5) do not include any description of establishment, undertaking or organisation excepted from those definitions by regulations.

(7) "Voluntary adoption agency" means an adoption society within the meaning of the Adoption Act 1976 which is a voluntary organisation within the meaning of that Act.

(8) Below in this Act—

(a) any reference to a description of establishment is a reference to a children's home, an independent hospital, an independent hospital in which treatment or nursing (or both) are provided for persons liable to be detained under the Mental Health Act 1983, an independent clinic, a care home or a residential family centre;

(b) a reference to any establishment is a reference to an establishment of any of those descriptions.

(9) Below in this Act—

(a) any reference to a description of agency is a reference to an independent medical agency, a domiciliary care agency, a nurses agency, a fostering agency or a voluntary adoption agency;

(b) a reference to any agency is a reference to an agency of any of those descriptions.

Registration authorities

5. For the purposes of this Act—

(a) the registration authority in relation to England is the National Care Standards Commission;

(b) the registration authority in relation to Wales is the National Assembly for Wales (referred to in this Act as "the Assembly").

Registration authorities.

6.—(1) There shall be a body corporate, to be known as the National Care Standards Commission (referred to in this Act as "the Commission"), which shall exercise in relation to England the functions conferred on it by or under this Act or any other enactment.

National Care Standards Commission.

(2) The Commission shall, in the exercise of its functions, act—

(a) in accordance with any directions in writing given to it by the Secretary of State; and

(b) under the general guidance of the Secretary of State.

(3) Schedule 1 shall have effect with respect to the Commission.

(4) The powers of the Secretary of State under this Part to give directions include power to give directions as to matters connected with the structure and organisation of the Commission, for example—

(a) directions about the establishment of offices for specified areas or regions;

(b) directions as to the organisation of staff into divisions.

7.—(1) The Commission shall have the general duty of keeping the Secretary of State informed about the provision in England of Part II services and, in particular, about—

General duties of the Commission.

(a) the availability of the provision; and

(b) the quality of the services.

(2) The Commission shall have the general duty of encouraging improvement in the quality of Part II services provided in England.

(3) The Commission shall make information about Part II services provided in England available to the public.

(4) When asked to do so by the Secretary of State, the Commission shall give the Secretary of State advice or information on such matters relating to the provision in England of Part II services as may be specified in the Secretary of State's request.

(5) The Commission may at any time give advice to the Secretary of State on—

(a) any changes which the Commission thinks should be made, for the purpose of securing improvement in the quality of Part II services provided in England, in the standards set out in statements under section 23; and

(b) any other matter connected with the provision in England of Part II services.

(6) The Secretary of State may by regulations confer additional functions on the Commission in relation to Part II services provided in England.

(7) In this section and section 8, "Part II services" means services of the kind provided by persons registered under Part II, other than the provision of—

 (a) medical or psychiatric treatment, or

 (b) listed services (as defined in section 2).

General functions of the Assembly.

8.—(1) The Assembly shall have the general duty of encouraging improvement in the quality of Part II services provided in Wales.

(2) The Assembly shall make information about Part II services provided in Wales available to the public.

(3) In relation to Part II services provided in Wales, the Assembly shall have any additional function specified in regulations made by the Assembly; but the regulations may only specify a function corresponding to a function which, by virtue of section 7, is exercisable by the Commission in relation to Part II services provided in England.

(4) The Assembly may charge a reasonable fee determined by it in connection with the exercise of any power conferred on it by or under this Act.

(5) The Assembly may provide training for the purpose of assisting persons to attain standards set out in any statements published by it under section 23.

Co-operative working.

9.—(1) The Commission for Health Improvement ("CHI") and the National Care Standards Commission ("NCSC") may, if authorised to do so by regulations, arrange—

 (a) for prescribed functions of the NCSC to be exercised by CHI on behalf of the NCSC;

 (b) for prescribed functions of CHI, so far as exercisable in relation to England, to be exercised by the NCSC on behalf of CHI,

and accordingly CHI and the NCSC each have power to exercise functions of the other in accordance with arrangements under this subsection.

(2) The Assembly and CHI may arrange for any functions of the Assembly mentioned in section 10(6) to be exercised by CHI on behalf of the Assembly; and accordingly CHI has power to exercise functions of the Assembly in accordance with arrangements under this subsection.

(3) The Assembly and CHI may, if authorised to do so by regulations, arrange for prescribed functions of CHI, so far as exercisable in relation to Wales, to be exercised by the Assembly on behalf of CHI; and accordingly the Assembly has power to exercise functions of CHI in accordance with arrangements under this subsection.

(4) References in this section to exercising functions include a reference to assisting with their exercise.

(5) Regulations under this section shall be made by the Secretary of State; but the Secretary of State may not make regulations under subsection (3) without the agreement of the Assembly.

Inquiries.

10.—(1) The Secretary of State may cause an inquiry to be held into any matter connected with the exercise by the Commission of its functions.

(2) The appropriate Minister may cause an inquiry to be held into any matter connected with a service provided in or by an establishment or agency.

(3) Before an inquiry is begun, the person causing the inquiry to be held may direct that it shall be held in private.

(4) Where no direction has been given, the person holding the inquiry may if he thinks fit hold it, or any part of it, in private.

(5) Subsections (2) to (5) of section 250 of the Local Government Act 1972 (powers in relation to local inquiries) shall apply in relation to an inquiry under this section as they apply in relation to a local inquiry under that section; and references in those provisions as so applied to a Minister shall be taken to include references to the Assembly.   1972 c. 70.

(6) Subsections (3) and (4) apply in relation to an inquiry under section 35 of the Government of Wales Act 1998 into any matter relevant to the exercise of—   1998 c. 38.

    (a) any functions exercisable by the Assembly by virtue of section 5(b) or 8(3); or

    (b) any other functions exercisable by the Assembly corresponding to functions exercisable by the Commission in relation to England,

as they apply in relation to an inquiry under this section.

(7) The report of the person who held the inquiry shall, unless the Minister who caused the inquiry to be held considers that there are exceptional circumstances which make it inappropriate to publish it, be published in a manner which that Minister considers appropriate.

PART II

ESTABLISHMENTS AND AGENCIES

Registration

11.—(1) Any person who carries on or manages an establishment or agency of any description without being registered under this Part in respect of it (as an establishment or, as the case may be, agency of that description) shall be guilty of an offence.   Requirement to register.

(2) Where the activities of an agency are carried on from two or more branches, each of those branches shall be treated as a separate agency for the purposes of this Part.

(3) The reference in subsection (1) to an agency does not include a reference to a voluntary adoption agency.

(4) The Secretary of State may by regulations make provision about the keeping of registers by the Commission for the purposes of this Part.

(5) A person guilty of an offence under this section shall be liable on summary conviction—

    (a) if subsection (6) does not apply, to a fine not exceeding level 5 on the standard scale;

    (b) if subsection (6) applies, to imprisonment for a term not exceeding six months, or to a fine not exceeding level 5 on the standard scale, or to both.

(6) This subsection applies if—

    (a) the person was registered in respect of the establishment or agency at a time before the commission of the offence but the registration was cancelled before the offence was committed; or

    (b) the conviction is a second or subsequent conviction of the offence and the earlier conviction, or one of the earlier convictions, was of an offence in relation to an establishment or agency of the same description.

Applications for registration.

12.—(1) A person seeking to be registered under this Part shall make an application to the registration authority.

(2) The application—

    (a) must give the prescribed information about prescribed matters;

    (b) must give any other information which the registration authority reasonably requires the applicant to give,

and must be accompanied by a fee of the prescribed amount.

(3) A person who applies for registration as the manager of an establishment or agency must be an individual.

(4) A person who carries on or manages, or wishes to carry on or manage, more than one establishment or agency must make a separate application in respect of each of them.

Grant or refusal of registration.

13.—(1) Subsections (2) to (4) apply where an application under section 12 has been made with respect to an establishment or agency in accordance with the provisions of this Part.

(2) If the registration authority is satisfied that—

    (a) the requirements of regulations under section 22; and

    (b) the requirements of any other enactment which appears to the registration authority to be relevant,

are being and will continue to be complied with (so far as applicable) in relation to the establishment or agency, it shall grant the application; otherwise it shall refuse it.

(3) The application may be granted either unconditionally or subject to such conditions as the registration authority thinks fit.

(4) On granting the application, the registration authority shall issue a certificate of registration to the applicant.

(5) The registration authority may at any time—

    (a) vary or remove any condition for the time being in force in relation to a person's registration; or

    (b) impose an additional condition.

Cancellation of registration.

14.—(1) The registration authority may at any time cancel the registration of a person in respect of an establishment or agency—

    (a) on the ground that that person has been convicted of a relevant offence;

    (b) on the ground that any other person has been convicted of such an offence in relation to the establishment or agency;

(c) on the ground that the establishment or agency is being, or has at any time been, carried on otherwise than in accordance with the relevant requirements;

(d) on any ground specified by regulations.

(2) For the purposes of this section the following are relevant offences—

(a) an offence under this Part or regulations made under it;

(b) an offence under the Registered Homes Act 1984 or regulations made under it;   1984 c. 23.

(c) an offence under the 1989 Act or regulations made under it;

(d) in relation to a voluntary adoption agency, an offence under regulations under section 9(2) of the Adoption Act 1976 or   1976 c. 36.
section 1(3) of the Adoption (Intercountry Aspects) Act 1999.   1999 c. 18.

(3) In this section "relevant requirements" means—

(a) any requirements or conditions imposed by or under this Part; and

(b) the requirements of any other enactment which appear to the registration authority to be relevant.

15.—(1) A person registered under this Part may apply to the   Applications by
registration authority—   registered persons.

(a) for the variation or removal of any condition for the time being in force in relation to the registration; or

(b) for the cancellation of the registration.

(2) But a person may not make an application under subsection (1)(b)—

(a) if the registration authority has given him notice under section 17(4)(a) of a proposal to cancel the registration, unless the registration authority has decided not to take that step; or

(b) if the registration authority has given him notice under section 19(3) of its decision to cancel the registration and the time within which an appeal may be brought has not expired or, if an appeal has been brought, it has not been determined.

(3) An application under subsection (1) shall be made in such manner and state such particulars as may be prescribed and, if made under paragraph (a) of that subsection, shall be accompanied by a fee of such amount as may be prescribed.

(4) If the registration authority decides to grant an application under subsection (1)(a) it shall serve notice in writing of its decision on the applicant (stating, where applicable, the condition as varied) and issue a new certificate of registration.

(5) If different amounts are prescribed under subsection (3), the regulations may provide for the registration authority to determine which amount is payable in a particular case.

16.—(1) Regulations may make provision about the registration of   Regulations about
persons under this Part in respect of establishments or agencies, and in   registration.
particular about—

(a) the making of applications for registration;

(b) the contents of certificates of registration.

(2) Regulations may provide that no application for registration under this Part may be made in respect of a fostering agency, or a voluntary adoption agency, which is an unincorporated body.

(3) Regulations may also require persons registered under this Part to pay to the registration authority an annual fee of such amount, and at such a time, as may be prescribed.

(4) A fee payable by virtue of this section may, without prejudice to any other method of recovery, be recovered summarily as a civil debt.

Registration procedure

Notice of proposals.

17.—(1) Subsections (2) and (3) apply where a person applies for registration in respect of an establishment or agency.

(2) If the registration authority proposes to grant the application subject to any conditions which have not been agreed in writing between it and the applicant, it shall give the applicant written notice of its proposal and of the conditions subject to which it proposes to grant his application.

(3) The registration authority shall give the applicant notice of a proposal to refuse the application.

(4) Except where it makes an application under section 20, the registration authority shall give any person registered in respect of an establishment or agency notice of a proposal—

(a) to cancel the registration (otherwise than in accordance with an application under section 15(1)(b));

(b) to vary or remove (otherwise than in accordance with an application under section 15(1)(a)) any condition for the time being in force in relation to the registration; or

(c) to impose any additional condition in relation to the registration.

(5) The registration authority shall give the applicant notice of a proposal to refuse an application under section 15(1)(a).

(6) A notice under this section shall give the registration authority's reasons for its proposal.

Right to make representations.

18.—(1) A notice under section 17 shall state that within 28 days of service of the notice any person on whom it is served may make written representations to the registration authority concerning any matter which that person wishes to dispute.

(2) Where a notice has been served under section 17, the registration authority shall not determine any matter to which the notice relates until either—

(a) any person on whom the notice was served has made written representations to it concerning the matter;

(b) any such person has notified the registration authority in writing that he does not intend to make representations; or

(c) the period during which any such person could have made representations has elapsed.

19.—(1) If the registration authority decides to grant an application for registration in respect of an establishment or agency unconditionally, or subject only to conditions which have been agreed in writing between it and the applicant, it shall give the applicant written notice of its decision.

(2) A notice under subsection (1) shall state the agreed conditions.

(3) If the registration authority decides to adopt a proposal under section 17, it shall serve notice in writing of its decision on any person on whom it was required to serve notice of the proposal.

(4) A notice under subsection (3) shall—

    (a) explain the right of appeal conferred by section 21;

    (b) in the case of a decision to adopt a proposal under section 17(2), state the conditions subject to which the application is granted; and

    (c) in the case of a decision to adopt a proposal under section 17(4)(b) or (c), state the condition as varied, the condition which is removed or (as the case may be) the additional condition imposed.

(5) Subject to subsection (6), a decision of the registration authority to adopt a proposal under section 17(2) or (4) shall not take effect—

    (a) if no appeal is brought, until the expiration of the period of 28 days referred to in section 21(2); and

    (b) if an appeal is brought, until it is determined or abandoned.

(6) Where, in the case of a decision to adopt a proposal under section 17(2), the applicant notifies the registration authority in writing before the expiration of the period mentioned in subsection (5)(a) that he does not intend to appeal, the decision shall take effect when the notice is served.

20.—(1) If—

    (a) the registration authority applies to a justice of the peace for an order—

        (i) cancelling the registration of a person in respect of an establishment or agency;

        (ii) varying or removing any condition for the time being in force by virtue of this Part; or

        (iii) imposing an additional condition; and

    (b) it appears to the justice that, unless the order is made, there will be a serious risk to a person's life, health or well-being,

the justice may make the order, and the cancellation, variation, removal or imposition shall have effect from the time when the order is made.

(2) An application under subsection (1) may, if the justice thinks fit, be made without notice.

(3) As soon as practicable after the making of an application under this section, the registration authority shall notify the appropriate authorities of the making of the application.

(4) An order under subsection (1) shall be in writing.

(5) Where such an order is made, the registration authority shall, as soon as practicable after the making of the order, serve on the person registered in respect of the establishment or agency—

(a) a copy of the order; and

(b) notice of the right of appeal conferred by section 21.

(6) For the purposes of this section the appropriate authorities are—

(a) the local authority in whose area the establishment or agency is situated;

(b) the Health Authority in whose area the establishment or agency is situated; and

(c) any statutory authority not falling within paragraph (a) or (b) whom the registration authority thinks it appropriate to notify.

(7) In this section "statutory authority" means a body established by or under an Act of Parliament.

Appeals to the Tribunal.

21.—(1) An appeal against—

(a) a decision of the registration authority under this Part; or

(b) an order made by a justice of the peace under section 20,

shall lie to the Tribunal.

(2) No appeal against a decision or order may be brought by a person more than 28 days after service on him of notice of the decision or order.

(3) On an appeal against a decision of the registration authority the Tribunal may confirm the decision or direct that it shall not have effect.

(4) On an appeal against an order made by a justice of the peace the Tribunal may confirm the order or direct that it shall cease to have effect.

(5) The Tribunal shall also have power on an appeal against a decision or order—

(a) to vary any condition for the time being in force in respect of the establishment or agency to which the appeal relates;

(b) to direct that any such condition shall cease to have effect; or

(c) to direct that any such condition as it thinks fit shall have effect in respect of the establishment or agency.

Regulations and standards

Regulation of establishments and agencies.

22.—(1) Regulations may impose in relation to establishments and agencies any requirements which the appropriate Minister thinks fit for the purposes of this Part and may in particular make any provision such as is mentioned in subsection (2), (7) or (8).

(2) Regulations may—

(a) make provision as to the persons who are fit to carry on or manage an establishment or agency;

(b) make provision as to the persons who are fit to work at an establishment or for the purposes of an agency;

(c) make provision as to the fitness of premises to be used as an establishment or for the purposes of an agency;

(d) make provision for securing the welfare of persons accommodated in an establishment or provided with services by an establishment, an independent medical agency or a domiciliary care agency;

(e) make provision for securing the welfare of children placed, under section 23(2)(a) of the 1989 Act, by a fostering agency;

(f) make provision as to the management and control of the operations of an establishment or agency;

(g) make provision as to the numbers of persons, or persons of any particular type, working at an establishment or for the purposes of an agency;

(h) make provision as to the management and training of such persons;

(i) impose requirements as to the financial position of an establishment or agency;

(j) make provision requiring the person carrying on an establishment or agency to appoint a manager in prescribed circumstances.

(3) Regulations under subsection (2)(a) may, in particular, make provision for prohibiting persons from managing an establishment or agency unless they are registered in, or in a particular part of, one of the registers maintained under section 56(1).

(4) Regulations under subsection (2)(b) may, in particular, make provision for prohibiting persons from working in such positions as may be prescribed at an establishment, or for the purposes of an agency, unless they are registered in, or in a particular part of, one of the registers maintained under section 56(1).

(5) Regulations under paragraph (d) of subsection (2) may, in particular, make provision—

(a) as to the promotion and protection of the health of persons such as are mentioned in that paragraph;

(b) as to the control and restraint of adults accommodated in, or provided with services by, an establishment;

(c) as to the control, restraint and discipline of children accommodated in, or provided with services by, an establishment.

(6) Regulations under paragraph (e) of subsection (2) may, in particular, make provision—

(a) as to the promotion and protection of the health of children such as are mentioned in that paragraph;

(b) as to the control, restraint and discipline of such children.

(7) Regulations may make provision as to the conduct of establishments and agencies, and such regulations may in particular—

(a) make provision as to the facilities and services to be provided in establishments and by agencies;

(b) make provision as to the keeping of accounts;

(c) make provision as to the keeping of documents and records;

(d) make provision as to the notification of events occurring in establishments or in premises used for the purposes of agencies;

    (e) make provision as to the giving of notice by the person carrying on an establishment or agency of periods during which he or (if he does not manage it himself) the manager proposes to be absent from the establishment or agency, and specify the information to be supplied in such a notice;

    (f) provide for the making of adequate arrangements for the running of an establishment or agency during a period when the manager is absent from it;

    (g) make provision as to the giving of notice by a person registered in respect of an establishment or agency of any intended change in the identity of the manager or the person carrying it on;

    (h) make provision as to the giving of notice by a person registered in respect of an establishment or agency which is carried on by a body corporate of changes in the ownership of the body or the identity of its officers;

    (i) make provision requiring the payment of a fee of such amount as may be prescribed in respect of any notification required to be made by virtue of paragraph (h);

    (j) make provision requiring arrangements to be made by the person who carries on, or manages, an establishment or agency for dealing with complaints made by or on behalf of those seeking, or receiving, any of the services provided in the establishment or by the agency and requiring that person to take steps for publicising the arrangements;

    (k) make provision requiring arrangements to be made by the person who carries on, or manages, an independent hospital, independent clinic or independent medical agency for securing that any medical or psychiatric treatment, or listed services, provided in or for the purposes of the establishment or (as the case may be) for the purposes of the agency are of appropriate quality and meet appropriate standards;

    (l) make provision requiring arrangements to be made by the person who carries on, or manages, a care home for securing that any nursing provided by the home is of appropriate quality and meets appropriate standards.

  (8) Regulations may make provision—

    (a) requiring the approval of the appropriate Minister for the provision and use of accommodation for the purpose of restricting the liberty of children in children's homes;

    (b) imposing other requirements (in addition to those imposed by section 25 of the 1989 Act (use of accommodation for restricting liberty)) as to the placing of a child in accommodation provided for the purpose mentioned in paragraph (a), including a requirement to obtain the permission of any local authority who are looking after the child;

    (c) as to the facilities which are to be provided for giving religious instruction to children in children's homes.

  (9) Before making regulations under this section, except regulations which amend other regulations made under this section and do not, in the opinion of the appropriate Minister, effect any substantial change in the provision made by those regulations, the appropriate Minister shall consult any persons he considers appropriate.

(10) References in this section to agencies do not include references to voluntary adoption agencies.

(11) In subsection (7)(k), "listed services" has the same meaning as in section 2.

23.—(1) The appropriate Minister may prepare and publish statements of national minimum standards applicable to establishments or agencies.

(2) The appropriate Minister shall keep the standards set out in the statements under review and may publish amended statements whenever he considers it appropriate to do so.

(3) Before issuing a statement, or an amended statement which in the opinion of the appropriate Minister effects a substantial change in the standards, the appropriate Minister shall consult any persons he considers appropriate.

(4) The standards shall be taken into account—

    (a) in the making of any decision by the registration authority under this Part;

    (b) in any proceedings for the making of an order under section 20;

    (c) in any proceedings on an appeal against such a decision or order; and

    (d) in any proceedings for an offence under regulations under this Part.

National minimum standards.

Offences

24. If a person registered in respect of an establishment or agency fails, without reasonable excuse, to comply with any condition for the time being in force by virtue of this Part in respect of the establishment or agency, he shall be guilty of an offence and liable on summary conviction to a fine not exceeding level 5 on the standard scale.

Failure to comply with conditions.

25.—(1) Regulations under this Part may provide that a contravention of or failure to comply with any specified provision of the regulations shall be an offence.

(2) A person guilty of an offence under the regulations shall be liable on summary conviction to a fine not exceeding level 4 on the standard scale.

Contravention of regulations.

26.—(1) A person who, with intent to deceive any person—

    (a) applies any name to premises in England or Wales; or

    (b) in any way describes such premises or holds such premises out,

so as to indicate, or reasonably be understood to indicate, that the premises are an establishment, or an agency, of a particular description shall be liable on summary conviction to a fine not exceeding level 5 on the standard scale unless registration has been effected under this Part in respect of the premises as an establishment or agency of that description.

(2) References to premises in subsection (1) shall be taken to include references to an undertaking or organisation.

(3) No person shall, with intent to deceive any person, in any way describe or hold out an establishment or agency as able to provide any

False descriptions of establishments and agencies.

service or do any thing the provision or doing of which would contravene a condition for the time being in force by virtue of this Part in respect of the establishment or agency.

(4) A person who contravenes subsection (3) shall be liable on summary conviction to a fine not exceeding level 5 on the standard scale.

False statements in applications.

27.—(1) Any person who, in an application for registration under this Part or for the variation of any condition in force in relation to his registration, knowingly makes a statement which is false or misleading in a material respect shall be guilty of an offence.

(2) A person guilty of an offence under this section shall be liable on summary conviction to a fine not exceeding level 4 on the standard scale.

Failure to display certificate of registration.

28.—(1) A certificate of registration issued under this Part in respect of any establishment or agency shall be kept affixed in a conspicuous place in the establishment or at the agency.

(2) If default is made in complying with subsection (1), any person registered in respect of the establishment or agency shall be guilty of an offence and liable on summary conviction to a fine not exceeding level 2 on the standard scale.

Proceedings for offences.

29.—(1) Proceedings in respect of an offence under this Part or regulations made under it shall not, without the written consent of the Attorney General, be taken by any person other than—

(a) the Commission or, in relation to any functions of the Commission which the Secretary of State is by virtue of section 113 for the time being discharging, the Secretary of State; or

(b) the Assembly.

(2) Proceedings for an offence under this Part or regulations made under it may be brought within a period of six months from the date on which evidence sufficient in the opinion of the prosecutor to warrant the proceedings came to his knowledge; but no such proceedings shall be brought by virtue of this subsection more than three years after the commission of the offence.

Offences by bodies corporate.

30.—(1) This section applies where any offence under this Part or regulations made under it is committed by a body corporate.

(2) If the offence is proved to have been committed with the consent or connivance of, or to be attributable to any neglect on the part of—

(a) any director, manager, or secretary of the body corporate; or

(b) any person who was purporting to act in any such capacity,

he (as well as the body corporate) shall be guilty of the offence and shall be liable to be proceeded against and punished accordingly.

(3) The reference in subsection (2) to a director, manager or secretary of a body corporate includes a reference—

(a) to any other similar officer of the body; and

(b) where the body is a local authority, to any officer or member of the authority.

Miscellaneous and supplemental

31.—(1) The registration authority may at any time require a person who carries on or manages an establishment or agency to provide it with any information relating to the establishment or agency which the registration authority considers it necessary or expedient to have for the purposes of its functions under this Part.

(2) A person authorised by the registration authority may at any time enter and inspect premises which are used, or which he has reasonable cause to believe to be used, as an establishment or for the purposes of an agency.

(3) A person authorised by virtue of this section to enter and inspect premises may—

    (a) make any examination into the state and management of the premises and treatment of patients or persons accommodated or cared for there which he thinks appropriate;

    (b) inspect and take copies of any documents or records (other than medical records) required to be kept in accordance with regulations under this Part, section 9(2) of the Adoption Act 1976, section 23(2)(a) or 59(2) of the 1989 Act or section 1(3) of the Adoption (Intercountry Aspects) Act 1999;

    (c) interview in private the manager or the person carrying on the establishment or agency;

    (d) interview in private any person employed there;

    (e) interview in private any patient or person accommodated or cared for there who consents to be interviewed.

(4) The powers under subsection (3)(b) include—

    (a) power to require the manager or the person carrying on the establishment or agency to produce any documents or records, wherever kept, for inspection on the premises; and

    (b) in relation to records which are kept by means of a computer, power to require the records to be produced in a form in which they are legible and can be taken away.

(5) Subsection (6) applies where the premises in question are used as an establishment and the person so authorised—

    (a) is a medical practitioner or registered nurse; and

    (b) has reasonable cause to believe that a patient or person accommodated or cared for there is not receiving proper care.

(6) The person so authorised may, with the consent of the person mentioned in subsection (5)(b), examine him in private and inspect any medical records relating to his treatment in the establishment.

The powers conferred by this subsection may be exercised in relation to a person who is incapable of giving consent without that person's consent.

(7) The Secretary of State may by regulations require the Commission to arrange for premises which are used as an establishment or for the purposes of an agency to be inspected on such occasions or at such intervals as may be prescribed.

(8) A person who proposes to exercise any power of entry or inspection conferred by this section shall if so required produce some duly authenticated document showing his authority to exercise the power.

(9) Any person who—

(a) intentionally obstructs the exercise of any power conferred by this section or section 32; or

(b) fails without a reasonable excuse to comply with any requirement under this section or that section,

shall be guilty of an offence and liable on summary conviction to a fine not exceeding level 4 on the standard scale.

Inspections: supplementary.

32.—(1) A person authorised by virtue of section 31 to enter and inspect any premises may seize and remove any document or other material or thing found there which he has reasonable grounds to believe may be evidence of a failure to comply with any condition or requirement imposed by or under this Part.

(2) A person so authorised—

(a) may require any person to afford him such facilities and assistance with respect to matters within the person's control as are necessary to enable him to exercise his powers under section 31 or this section;

(b) may take such measurements and photographs and make such recordings as he considers necessary to enable him to exercise those powers.

(3) A person authorised by virtue of section 31 to inspect any records shall be entitled to have access to, and to check the operation of, any computer and any associated apparatus which is or has been in use in connection with the records in question.

(4) The references in section 31 to the person carrying on the establishment or agency include, in the case of an establishment or agency which is carried on by a company, a reference to any director, manager, secretary or other similar officer of the company.

(5) Where any premises which are used as an establishment or for the purposes of an agency have been inspected under section 31, the registration authority—

(a) shall prepare a report on the matters inspected; and

(b) shall without delay send a copy of the report to each person who is registered in respect of the establishment or agency.

(6) The registration authority shall make copies of any report prepared under subsection (5) available for inspection at its offices by any person at any reasonable time; and may take any other steps for publicising a report which it considers appropriate.

(7) Any person who asks the registration authority for a copy of a report prepared under subsection (5) shall be entitled to have one on payment of a reasonable fee determined by the registration authority; but nothing in this subsection prevents the registration authority from providing a copy free of charge when it considers it appropriate to do so.

(8) Where the Secretary of State has specified regions in a direction made under paragraph 9 of Schedule 1, the reference in subsection (6) to

offices is, in relation to premises in England which are used as an establishment or for the purposes of an agency, a reference to the Commission's offices for the region in which the premises are situated.

33.—(1) Regulations may require the person carrying on an establishment or agency to make an annual return to the registration authority.

Annual returns.

(2) Provision may be made by the regulations as to the contents of the return and the period in respect of which and date by which it is to be made.

34.—(1) Regulations may—

Liquidators etc.

   (a) require any person to whom this section applies to give notice of his appointment to the registration authority;

   (b) require any person to whom this section applies to appoint a person to manage the establishment or agency in question.

(2) This section applies to any person appointed as—

   (a) a receiver or manager of the property of a relevant company;

   (b) the liquidator or provisional liquidator of a relevant company; or

   (c) the trustee in bankruptcy of a relevant individual.

(3) In this section—

"company" includes a partnership;

"relevant company" means a company which is registered under this Part in respect of an establishment or agency; and

"relevant individual" means an individual who is registered under this Part in respect of an establishment or agency.

35.—(1) Regulations may—

Death of registered person.

   (a) provide for the provisions of this Part to apply with prescribed modifications in cases where a person who was the only person registered under this Part in respect of an establishment or agency has died;

   (b) require the personal representatives of a deceased person who was registered in respect of an establishment or agency to notify the registration authority of his death.

(2) Regulations under subsection (1)(a) may in particular—

   (a) provide for the establishment or agency to be carried on for a prescribed period by a person who is not registered in respect of it; and

   (b) include provision for the prescribed period to be extended by such further period as the registration authority may allow.

36.—(1) Subject to subsection (3), the registration authority shall secure that copies of any register kept for the purposes of this Part are available at its offices for inspection at all reasonable times by any person.

Provision of copies of registers.

(2) Subject to subsections (3) and (4), any person who asks the registration authority for a copy of, or of an extract from, a register kept for the purposes of this Part shall be entitled to have one.

(3) Regulations may provide that subsections (1) and (2) shall not apply—

    (a) in such circumstances as may be prescribed; or

    (b) to such parts of a register as may be prescribed.

(4) A fee determined by the registration authority shall be payable for the copy except—

    (a) in prescribed circumstances;

    (b) in any other case where the registration authority considers it appropriate to provide the copy free of charge.

Service of documents.

37.—(1) Any notice or other document required under this Part to be served on a person carrying on or managing, or intending to carry on or manage, an establishment or agency may be served on him—

    (a) by being delivered personally to him; or

    (b) by being sent by post to him in a registered letter or by the recorded delivery service at his proper address.

1978 c. 30.

(2) For the purposes of section 7 of the Interpretation Act 1978 (which defines "service by post") a letter addressed to a person carrying on or managing an establishment or agency enclosing a notice or other document under this Act shall be deemed to be properly addressed if it is addressed to him at the establishment or agency.

(3) Where a notice or other document is served as mentioned in subsection (1)(b), the service shall, unless the contrary is proved, be deemed to have been effected on the third day after the day on which it is sent.

(4) Any notice or other document required to be served on a body corporate or a firm shall be duly served if it is served on the secretary or clerk of that body or a partner of that firm.

(5) For the purposes of this section, and of section 7 of the Interpretation Act 1978 in its application to this section, without prejudice to subsection (2) above, the proper address of a person shall be—

    (a) in the case of a secretary or clerk of a body corporate, that of the registered or principal office of that body;

    (b) in the case of a partner of a firm, that of the principal office of the firm; and

    (c) in any other case, the last known address of the person.

Transfers of staff under Part II.

38.—(1) The appropriate Minister may by order make a scheme for the transfer to the new employer of any eligible employee.

(2) In this section—

    "eligible employee" means a person who is employed under a contract of employment with an old employer on work which would have continued but for the provisions of this Part;

    "new employer" means the registration authority;

    "old employer" means a local authority or a Health Authority.

39. In section 21 of the Registered Homes Act 1984 (meaning of nursing home)—

    (a) in subsection (1), after "(3)" there is inserted "and (3A)";

    (b) in subsection (2), for "subsection (1) above" there is substituted "this section";

    (c) in subsection (3)(e)(ii), "dental practitioner or" is omitted; and

    (d) after subsection (3) there is inserted—

Temporary extension of meaning of "nursing home".

1984 c. 23.

"(3A) The definition in subsection (1) above does not include any premises used, or intended to be used, wholly or mainly by a dental practitioner for the purpose of treating his patients unless subsection (3B) or (3C) below applies.

(3B) This subsection applies if—

    (a) the premises are also used, or intended to be used, by that or another dental practitioner for the purpose of treating his patients under general anaesthesia; and

    (b) the premises are not used, or intended to be used, by any dental practitioner for the purpose of treating his patients under general anaesthesia—

        (i) in pursuance of the National Health Service Act 1977; or

        (ii) under an agreement made in accordance with Part I of the National Health Service (Primary Care) Act 1997.

1977 c. 49.

1997 c. 46.

(3C) This subsection applies if the premises are used, or intended to be used, for the provision of treatment by specially controlled techniques and are not excepted by regulations under subsection (3)(g) above."

40. In section 63(3)(a) of the 1989 Act (meaning of "children's home"), for "more than three children at any one time" there shall be substituted "children".

Temporary extension of meaning of "children's home".

41.—(1) In paragraph 1(4) of Schedule 5 to the 1989 Act (voluntary homes and voluntary organisations)—

    (a) in paragraph (a), after "is not" there shall be inserted ", or has not been,";

    (b) after "is" there shall be inserted ", or has been,".

Children's homes: temporary provision about cancellation of registration.

(2) In paragraph 2 of that Schedule, after sub-paragraph (5) there shall be inserted—

"(6) In relation to a home which has ceased to exist, the reference in sub-paragraph (4) to any person carrying on the home shall be taken to be a reference to each of the persons who carried it on."

(3) In paragraph 3(3) of Schedule 6 to the 1989 Act (registered children's homes), after "is being" there shall be inserted "and has been".

(4) In paragraph 4 of that Schedule—

    (a) in sub-paragraph (3) after "is being" there shall be inserted ", or has been,";

    (b) after sub-paragraph (4) there shall be inserted—

"(5) In relation to a home which has ceased to exist, references in this paragraph and paragraph 5(4) to the person, or any person, carrying on the home include references to each of the persons who carried it on."

Power to extend
the application of
Part II.

42.—(1) Regulations may provide for the provisions of this Part to apply, with such modifications as may be specified in the regulations, to prescribed persons to whom subsection (2) or (3) applies.

(2) This subsection applies to—

> (a) local authorities providing services in the exercise of their social services functions; and

> (b) persons who provide services which are similar to services which—

>> (i) may or must be so provided by local authorities; or

>> (ii) may or must be provided by Health Authorities, Special Health Authorities, NHS trusts or Primary Care Trusts.

(3) This subsection applies to persons who carry on or manage an undertaking (other than an establishment or agency) which consists of or includes supplying, or providing services for the purpose of supplying, individuals mentioned in subsection (4).

(4) The individuals referred to in subsection (3) are those who provide services for the purpose of any of the services mentioned in subsection (2).

PART III

LOCAL AUTHORITY SERVICES

Introductory.

43.—(1) This section has effect for the purposes of this Part.

(2) "Relevant functions", in relation to a local authority, means relevant adoption functions and relevant fostering functions.

(3) In relation to a local authority—

> (a) "relevant adoption functions" means functions under the Adoption Act 1976 of making or participating in arrangements for the adoption of children; and

1976 c. 36.

> (b) "relevant fostering functions" means functions under section 23(2)(a) of the 1989 Act or regulations under any of paragraphs (a), (b) or (d) to (f) of paragraph 12 of Schedule 2 to that Act.

General powers of
the Commission.

44. The Commission may at any time give advice to the Secretary of State on—

> (a) any changes which the Commission thinks should be made, for the purpose of securing improvement in the quality of services provided by local authorities in England in the exercise of relevant functions, in the standards set out in statements under section 49; and

> (b) any other matter connected with the exercise by local authorities in England of relevant functions.

Part III
Inspection by
registration
authority of
adoption and
fostering services.

45.—(1) Subject to section 47(6)—

    (a) the registration authority may at any time require a local authority to provide it with any information relating to the discharge by the local authority of relevant functions which the registration authority considers it necessary or expedient to have for the purposes of its functions under this Part;

    (b) a person authorised to do so by the registration authority may at any time enter and inspect premises which are used, or which he has reasonable cause to believe to be used, by a local authority in its discharge of relevant functions.

(2) A person authorised by virtue of this section to enter and inspect premises may—

    (a) inspect and take copies of any documents or records relating to the discharge by the local authority of relevant functions;

    (b) interview in private any employee of the local authority.

(3) The powers under subsection (2)(a) include—

    (a) power to require the local authority to produce any documents or records, wherever kept, for inspection on the premises; and

    (b) in relation to records which are kept by means of a computer, power to require the records to be produced in a form in which they are legible and can be taken away.

(4) Subject to section 47(6), the Secretary of State may by regulations require the Commission to arrange for premises which are used by a local authority in its discharge of relevant functions to be inspected on such occasions or at such intervals as may be prescribed.

(5) Subsections (8) and (9) of section 31 shall have effect as if any reference in them to section 31 included a reference to this section and section 46.

46.—(1) A person authorised by virtue of section 45 to enter and inspect any premises may seize and remove any document or other material or thing found there which he has reasonable grounds to believe may be evidence of a failure to comply with the regulatory requirements.

(2) A person so authorised—

    (a) may require any person to afford him such facilities and assistance with respect to matters within the person's control as are necessary to enable him to exercise his powers under section 45 or this section;

    (b) may take such measurements and photographs and make such recordings as he considers necessary to enable him to exercise those powers.

(3) A person authorised by virtue of section 45 to inspect any records shall be entitled to have access to, and to check the operation of, any computer and any associated apparatus or material which is or has been in use in connection with the records in question.

(4) Where any premises which are used by a local authority in its discharge of relevant functions have been inspected under section 45, the registration authority—

(a) shall prepare a report on the discharge by the local authority of relevant functions; and

(b) shall without delay send a copy of the report to the local authority.

(5) The registration authority shall make copies of any report prepared under subsection (4) available for inspection at its offices by any person at any reasonable time; and may take any other steps for publicising a report which it considers appropriate.

(6) Any person who asks the registration authority for a copy of the report shall be entitled to have one on payment of a reasonable fee determined by the registration authority; but nothing in this subsection prevents the registration authority from providing a copy free of charge when it considers it appropriate to do so.

(7) In this section and section 47 "the regulatory requirements" means the requirements of regulations under—

(a) section 48;

(b) section 23(2)(a) of the 1989 Act (regulations about the placing of children with foster parents);

1976 c. 36.

(c) section 9(3) of the Adoption Act 1976 (regulation of adoption agencies); and

1999 c. 18.

(d) section 1(1) of the Adoption (Intercountry Aspects) Act 1999 (regulations giving effect to the Convention on Protection of Children and Co-operation in respect of Intercountry Adoption).

(8) Where the Secretary of State has specified regions in a direction made under paragraph 9 of Schedule 1, the reference in subsection (5) to offices is, in relation to premises in England which are used by a local authority in its discharge of relevant functions, a reference to the Commission's offices for the region in which the premises are situated.

Action following inspection.

47.—(1) If the Commission considers at any time—

(a) that the discharge by a local authority of relevant functions fails to satisfy the regulatory requirements; and

(b) that the failure is substantial,

it shall report that fact to the Secretary of State.

(2) Subsections (3) and (4) apply in relation to a local authority where—

(a) a person authorised by the Commission has exercised in relation to the authority any power conferred by section 45(1)(b); or

(b) the Commission has given the authority a notice under subsection (5) and the time specified (in accordance with paragraph (b) of that subsection) in the notice has expired.

(3) If the Commission considers that the discharge by the authority of relevant functions satisfies the regulatory requirements, it shall report that fact to the Secretary of State.

(4) If the Commission considers that the discharge by the authority of relevant functions fails to satisfy the regulatory requirements, but that the failure is not substantial, the Commission shall—

(a) report that fact to the Secretary of State; or

(b) if it considers that it is not appropriate to make a report under paragraph (a), give the authority a notice under subsection (5) and inform the Secretary of State that it has done so.

(5) A notice under this subsection is a notice which—

(a) specifies the respects in which the Commission considers that the discharge by the authority of relevant functions fails to satisfy the regulatory requirements and any action which the Commission considers the authority should take to remedy the failure; and

(b) specifies the time by which the failure should be remedied.

(6) Where the Commission has made a report to the Secretary of State under subsection (1) or (4)(a), the powers conferred by section 45(1) shall not be exercisable in relation to the authority concerned at any time unless the Secretary of State has notified the Commission that this subsection has ceased to apply.

48.—(1) Regulations may make provision about the exercise by local authorities of relevant fostering functions, and may in particular make provision—

> Regulation of the exercise of relevant fostering functions.

(a) as to the persons who are fit to work for local authorities in connection with the exercise of such functions;

(b) as to the fitness of premises to be used by local authorities in their exercise of such functions;

(c) as to the management and control of the operations of local authorities in their exercise of such functions;

(d) as to the numbers of persons, or persons of any particular type, working for local authorities in connection with the exercise of such functions;

(e) as to the management and training of such persons.

(2) Regulations under subsection (1)(a) may, in particular, make provision for prohibiting persons from working for local authorities in such positions as may be prescribed unless they are registered in, or in a particular part of, one of the registers maintained under section 56(1).

49.—(1) Subsections (1), (2) and (3) of section 23 shall apply to local authorities in their exercise of relevant functions as they apply to establishments and agencies.

> National minimum standards.

(2) The standards shall be taken into account in the making of any decision under section 47.

50.—(1) Regulations may require a local authority to make to the registration authority an annual return containing such information with respect to the exercise by the local authority of relevant functions as may be prescribed.

> Annual returns.

(2) Provision may be made by the regulations as to the period in respect of which and date by which the return is to be made.

Annual fee.

51.—(1) Regulations may require any local authority in relation to which powers conferred by section 45(1) may be exercised to pay to the registration authority an annual fee of such amount, and at such a time, as may be prescribed.

(2) A fee payable by virtue of this section may, without prejudice to any other method of recovery, be recovered summarily as a civil debt.

Contravention of regulations.

52.—(1) Regulations under this Part may provide that a contravention of or failure to comply with any specified provision of the regulations shall be an offence.

(2) A person guilty of an offence under the regulations shall be liable on summary conviction to a fine not exceeding level 4 on the standard scale.

Offences: general provisions.

53. Sections 29 and 30 apply in relation to this Part as they apply in relation to Part II.

PART IV

SOCIAL CARE WORKERS

Preliminary

Care Councils.

54.—(1) There shall be—

    (a) a body corporate to be known as the General Social Care Council (referred to in this Act as "the English Council"); and

    (b) a body corporate to be known as the Care Council for Wales or Cyngor Gofal Cymru (referred to in this Act as "the Welsh Council"),

which shall have the functions conferred on them by or under this Act or any other enactment.

(2) It shall be the duty of the English Council to promote in relation to England—

    (a) high standards of conduct and practice among social care workers; and

    (b) high standards in their training.

(3) It shall be the duty of the Welsh Council to promote in relation to Wales—

    (a) high standards of conduct and practice among social care workers; and

    (b) high standards in their training.

(4) Each Council shall, in the exercise of its functions, act—

    (a) in accordance with any directions given to it by the appropriate Minister; and

    (b) under the general guidance of the appropriate Minister.

(5) Directions under subsection (4) shall be given in writing.

(6) Schedule 1 shall have effect with respect to a Council.

(7) In this Act, references to a Council are—

    (a) in relation to England, a reference to the General Social Care Council,

    (b) in relation to Wales, a reference to the Care Council for Wales.

55.—(1) This section has effect for the purposes of this Part.   Interpretation.

(2) "Social care worker" means a person (other than a person excepted by regulations) who—

    (a) engages in relevant social work (referred to in this Part as a "social worker");

    (b) is employed at a children's home, care home or residential family centre or for the purposes of a domiciliary care agency, a fostering agency or a voluntary adoption agency;

    (c) manages an establishment, or an agency, of a description mentioned in paragraph (b); or

    (d) is supplied by a domiciliary care agency to provide personal care in their own homes for persons who by reason of illness, infirmity or disability are unable to provide it for themselves without assistance.

(3) Regulations may provide that persons of any of the following descriptions shall be treated as social care workers—

    (a) a person engaged in work for the purposes of a local authority's social services functions, or in the provision of services similar to services which may or must be provided by local authorities in the exercise of those functions;

    (b) a person engaged in the provision of personal care for any person;

    (c) a person who manages, or is employed in, an undertaking (other than an establishment or agency) which consists of or includes supplying, or providing services for the purpose of supplying, persons to provide personal care;

    (d) a person employed in connection with the discharge of functions of the appropriate Minister under section 80 of the 1989 Act (inspection of children's homes etc.);

    (e) staff of the Commission or the Assembly who—

        (i) inspect premises under section 87 of the 1989 Act (welfare of children accommodated in independent schools and colleges) or section 31 or 45 of this Act; or

        (ii) are responsible for persons who do so;

      and staff of the Assembly who inspect premises under section 79T of that Act (inspection of child minding and day care in Wales) or are responsible for persons who do so;

    (f) a person employed in a day centre;

    (g) a person participating in a course approved by a Council under section 63 for persons wishing to become social workers.

(4) "Relevant social work" means social work which is required in connection with any health, education or social services provided by any person.

PART IV

(5) "Day centre" means a place where nursing or personal care (but not accommodation) is provided wholly or mainly for persons mentioned in section 3(2).

Registration

The register.

56.—(1) Each Council shall maintain a register of—

(a) social workers; and

(b) social care workers of any other description specified by the appropriate Minister by order.

(2) There shall be a separate part of the register for social workers and for each description of social care workers so specified.

(3) The appropriate Minister may by order provide for a specified part of the register to be closed, as from a date specified by the order, so that on or after that date no further persons can become registered in that part.

(4) The appropriate Minister shall consult the Council before making, varying or revoking any order under this section.

Applications for registration.

57.—(1) An application for registration under this Part shall be made to the Council in accordance with rules made by it.

(2) An application under subsection (1) shall specify each part of the register in which registration is sought and such other matters as may be required by the rules.

Grant or refusal of registration.

58.—(1) If the Council is satisfied that the applicant—

(a) is of good character;

(b) is physically and mentally fit to perform the whole or part of the work of persons registered in any part of the register to which his application relates; and

(c) satisfies the following conditions,

it shall grant the application, either unconditionally or subject to such conditions as it thinks fit; and in any other case it shall refuse it.

(2) The first condition is that—

(a) in the case of an applicant for registration as a social worker—

(i) he has successfully completed a course approved by the Council under section 63 for persons wishing to become social workers;

(ii) he satisfies the requirements of section 64; or

(iii) he satisfies any requirements as to training which the Council may by rules impose in relation to social workers;

(b) in the case of an applicant for registration as a social care worker of any other description, he satisfies any requirements as to training which the Council may by rules impose in relation to social care workers of that description.

(3) The second condition is that the applicant satisfies any requirements as to conduct and competence which the Council may by rules impose.

59.—(1) Each Council shall by rules determine circumstances in which, and the means by which—

    (a) a person may be removed from a part of the register, whether or not for a specified period;

    (b) a person who has been removed from a part of the register may be restored to that part;

    (c) a person's registration in a part of the register may be suspended for a specified period;

    (d) the suspension of a person's registration in a part of the register may be terminated;

    (e) an entry in a part of the register may be removed, altered or restored.

(2) The rules shall make provision as to the procedure to be followed, and the rules of evidence to be observed, in proceedings brought for the purposes of the rules, whether before the Council or any committee of the Council.

(3) The rules shall provide for such proceedings to be in public except in such cases (if any) as the rules may specify.

(4) Where a person's registration in a part of the register is suspended under subsection (1)(c), he shall be treated as not being registered in that part notwithstanding that his name still appears in it.

60. A Council may by rules make provision about the registration of persons under this Part and, in particular—

    (a) as to the keeping of the register;

    (b) as to the documentary and other evidence to be produced by those applying for registration or for additional qualifications to be recorded, or for any entry in the register to be altered or restored;

    (c) for a person's registration to remain effective without limitation of time (subject to removal from the register in accordance with rules made by virtue of section 59) or to lapse after a specified period or in specified cases, or to be subject to renewal as and when provided by the rules.

61.—(1) If a person who is not registered as a social worker in any relevant register with intent to deceive another—

    (a) takes or uses the title of social worker;

    (b) takes or uses any title or description implying that he is so registered, or in any way holds himself out as so registered,

he is guilty of an offence.

(2) For the purposes of subsection (1), a register is a relevant register if it is—

    (a) maintained by a Council; or

    (b) a prescribed register maintained under a provision of the law of Scotland or Northern Ireland which appears to the appropriate Minister to correspond to the provisions of this Part.

(3) A person guilty of an offence under this section shall be liable on summary conviction to a fine not exceeding level 5 on the standard scale.

Codes of practice

Codes of practice.

62.—(1) Each Council shall prepare and from time to time publish codes of practice laying down—

(a) standards of conduct and practice expected of social care workers; and

(b) standards of conduct and practice in relation to social care workers, being standards expected of persons employing or seeking to employ them.

(2) The Council shall—

(a) keep the codes under review; and

(b) vary their provisions whenever it considers it appropriate to do so.

(3) Before issuing or varying a code, a Council shall consult any persons it considers appropriate to consult.

(4) A code published by a Council shall be taken into account—

(a) by the Council in making a decision under this Part; and

(b) in any proceedings on an appeal against such a decision.

(5) Local authorities making any decision about the conduct of any social care workers employed by them shall, if directed to do so by the appropriate Minister, take into account any code published by the Council.

(6) Any person who asks a Council for a copy of a code shall be entitled to have one.

Training

Approval of courses etc.

63.—(1) Each Council may, in accordance with rules made by it, approve courses in relevant social work for persons who are or wish to become social workers.

(2) An approval given under this section may be either unconditional or subject to such conditions as the Council thinks fit.

(3) Rules made by virtue of this section may in particular make provision—

(a) about the content of, and methods of completing, courses;

(b) as to the provision to the Council of information about courses;

(c) as to the persons who may participate in courses, or in parts of courses specified in the rules;

(d) as to the numbers of persons who may participate in courses;

(e) for the award by the Council of certificates of the successful completion of courses;

(f) about the lapse and renewal of approvals; and

(g) about the withdrawal of approvals.

(4) A Council may—

(a) conduct, or make arrangements for the conduct of, examinations in connection with such courses as are mentioned in this section or section 67; and

(b) carry out, or assist other persons in carrying out, research into matters relevant to training for relevant social work.

(5) A course for persons who wish to become social workers shall not be approved under this section unless the Council considers that it is such as to enable persons completing it to attain the required standard of proficiency in relevant social work.

(6) In subsection (5) "the required standard of proficiency in relevant social work" means the standard described in rules made by the Council.

(7) The Council shall from time to time publish a list of the courses which are approved under this section.

64.—(1) An applicant for registration as a social worker in the register maintained by the English Council satisfies the requirements of this section if—

> (a) being a national of any EEA State—
>
> > (i) he has professional qualifications, obtained in an EEA State other than the United Kingdom, which the Secretary of State has by order designated as having Community equivalence for the purposes of such registration; and
> >
> > (ii) he satisfies any other requirements which the Council may by rules impose; or
>
> (b) he has, elsewhere than in England, undergone training in relevant social work and either—
>
> > (i) that training is recognised by the Council as being to a standard sufficient for such registration; or
> >
> > (ii) it is not so recognised, but the applicant has undergone in England or elsewhere such additional training as the Council may require.

Qualifications gained outside a Council's area.

(2) An applicant for registration as a social worker in the register maintained by the Welsh Council satisfies the requirements of this section if—

> (a) being a national of any EEA State—
>
> > (i) he has professional qualifications, obtained in an EEA State other than the United Kingdom, which the Assembly has by order designated as having Community equivalence for the purposes of such registration; and
> >
> > (ii) he satisfies any other requirements which the Council may by rules impose; or
>
> (b) he has, elsewhere than in Wales, undergone training in relevant social work and either—
>
> > (i) that training is recognised by the Council as being to a standard sufficient for such registration; or
> >
> > (ii) it is not so recognised, but the applicant has undergone in Wales or elsewhere such additional training as the Council may require.

(3) An order under subsection (1)(a) or (2)(a) may provide that a professional qualification designated by the order is to be regarded as having Community equivalence for the purposes of registration as a social worker in the register maintained by the English or, as the case may be, Welsh Council only if prescribed conditions required by a directive

issued by the Council of the European Communities are fulfilled; and different conditions may be prescribed with respect to the same qualification for different circumstances.

(4) Any person who—

(a) is not a national of an EEA State; but

(b) is, by virtue of a right conferred by Article 11 of Council Regulation (EEC) No. 1612/68 (on freedom of movement for workers within the Community) or any other enforceable Community right, entitled to be treated, as regards the right to engage in relevant social work, no less favourably than a national of such a State,

shall be treated for the purposes of subsection (1)(a) or (2)(a) as if he were such a national.

(5) In this section—

"EEA State" means a Contracting Party to the EEA Agreement;

"EEA Agreement" means the Agreement on the European Economic Area signed at Oporto on 2nd May 1992 as adjusted by the Protocol signed at Brussels on 17th March 1993;

"national", in relation to an EEA State, means the same as it does for the purposes of the Community Treaties.

Post registration training.

65.—(1) A Council may make rules requiring persons registered under this Part in any part of the register to undertake further training.

(2) The rules may, in particular, make provision with respect to persons who fail to comply with any requirements of rules made by the Council, including provision for their registration to cease to have effect.

(3) Before making, or varying, any rules by virtue of this section the Council shall take such steps as are reasonably practicable to consult the persons who are registered in the relevant part of the register and such other persons as the Council considers appropriate.

Visitors for certain social work courses.

66.—(1) A Council may by rules make provision for the visiting of places at which or institutions by which or under whose direction—

(a) any relevant course (or part of such a course) is, or is proposed to be, given; or

(b) any examination is, or is proposed to be, held in connection with any relevant course.

(2) The rules may make provision—

(a) for the appointment of visitors;

(b) for reports to be made by visitors on—

(i) the nature and quality of the instruction given, or to be given, and the facilities provided or to be provided, at the place or by the institution visited; and

(ii) such other matters as may be specified in the rules;

(c) for the payment by the Council of fees, allowances and expenses to persons appointed as visitors;

(d) for such persons to be treated, for the purposes of Schedule 1, as members of the Council's staff.

(3) In subsection (1) "relevant course", in relation to a Council, means—

    (a) any course for which approval by the Council has been given, or is being sought, under section 63; or

    (b) any training which a person admitted to the part for social workers of the register maintained by the Council may be required to undergo after registration.

67.—(1) The appropriate Minister has the function of—

    (a) ascertaining what training is required by persons who are or wish to become social care workers;

    (b) ascertaining what financial and other assistance is required for promoting such training;

    (c) encouraging the provision of such assistance;

    (d) drawing up occupational standards for social care workers.

Functions of the appropriate Minister.

(2) The appropriate Minister shall encourage persons to take part in courses approved by a Council under section 63 and other courses relevant to the training of persons who are or wish to become social care workers.

(3) If it appears to the appropriate Minister that adequate provision is not being made for training persons who are or wish to become social care workers, the appropriate Minister may provide, or secure the provision of, courses for that purpose.

(4) The appropriate Minister may, upon such terms and subject to such conditions as the Minister considers appropriate—

    (a) make grants, and pay travelling and other allowances, to persons resident in England and Wales, in order to secure their training in the work of social care workers;

    (b) make grants to organisations providing training in the work of social care workers.

(5) Any functions of the Secretary of State under this section—

    (a) may be delegated by him to the English Council; or

    (b) may be exercised by any person, or by employees of any person, authorised to do so by the Secretary of State.

(6) Any functions of the Assembly under this section—

    (a) may be delegated by the Assembly to the Welsh Council; or

    (b) may be exercised by any person, or by employees of any person, authorised to do so by the Assembly.

(7) For the purpose of determining—

    (a) the terms and effect of an authorisation under subsection (5)(b) or (6)(b); and

(b) the effect of so much of any contract made between the appropriate Minister and the authorised person as relates to the exercise of the function,

1994 c. 40.

Part II of the Deregulation and Contracting Out Act 1994 shall have effect as if the authorisation were given by virtue of an order under section 69 of that Act and, in respect of an authorisation given by the Assembly, references to a Minister included the Assembly; and in subsection (5)(b) and (6)(b) "employee" has the same meaning as in that Part.

Miscellaneous and supplemental

Appeals to the Tribunal.

68.—(1) An appeal against a decision of a Council under this Part in respect of registration shall lie to the Tribunal.

(2) On an appeal against a decision, the Tribunal may confirm the decision or direct that it shall not have effect.

(3) The Tribunal shall also have power on an appeal against a decision—

(a) to vary any condition for the time being in force in respect of the person to whom the appeal relates;

(b) to direct that any such condition shall cease to have effect; or

(c) to direct that any such condition as it thinks fit shall have effect in respect of that person.

Publication etc. of register.

69.—(1) A Council shall publish the register maintained by it in such manner, and at such times, as it considers appropriate.

(2) Any person who asks the Council for a copy of, or of an extract from, the register shall be entitled to have one.

Abolition of Central Council for Education and Training in Social Work.
1983 c. 41.

70.—(1) The Central Council for Education and Training in Social Work (referred to in this Act as "CCETSW") shall cease to exercise in relation to England and Wales the functions conferred on it by or under section 10 of the Health and Social Services and Social Security Adjudications Act 1983.

(2) Her Majesty may by Order in Council make a scheme under subsection (3), or make any provision under subsection (4), which She considers necessary or expedient in consequence of the functions of CCETSW referred to in subsection (1) ceasing, by virtue of that subsection, an Act of the Scottish Parliament or an Act of the Northern Ireland Assembly, to be exercisable in relation to any part of the United Kingdom.

(3) A scheme may provide—

(a) for the transfer to the new employer of any eligible employee;

(b) for the transfer to any person of any property belonging to CCETSW;

(c) for any person to have such rights and interests in relation to any property belonging to CCETSW as Her Majesty considers appropriate (whether in connection with a transfer or otherwise);

(d) for the transfer to any person of any liabilities of CCETSW.

(4) The Order in Council may make—

(a) any supplementary, incidental or consequential provision;

(b) any transitory, transitional or saving provision,

including provision amending Schedule 3 to that Act or repealing that Schedule, section 10 of that Act and any reference in any enactment to CCETSW.

(5) In this section—

"eligible employee" means a person who is employed under a contract of employment with the old employer;

"new employer" means—

(a) in relation to England or Wales, the Council;

(b) in relation to Scotland or Northern Ireland, any body established under a provision of the law of Scotland or (as the case may be) Northern Ireland which appears to Her Majesty to perform functions corresponding to those of a Council;

"old employer" means CCETSW;

"property" includes rights and interests of any description.

71.—(1) Any power of a Council to make rules under this Part may be exercised— Rules.

(a) either in relation to all cases to which the power extends, or in relation to all those cases subject to specified exceptions, or in relation to any specified cases or classes of case; and

(b) so as to make, as respects the cases in relation to which it is exercised, the same provision for all cases in relation to which the power is exercised, or different provision for different cases or different classes of case, or different provision as respects the same case or class of case for different purposes.

(2) Rules made by a Council under this Part may make provision for the payment of reasonable fees to the Council in connection with the discharge of the Council's functions.

(3) In particular, the rules may make provision for the payment of such fees in connection with—

(a) registration (including applications for registration or for amendment of the register);

(b) the approval of courses under section 63;

(c) the provision of training;

(d) the provision of copies of codes of practice or copies of, or extracts from, the register,

including provision requiring persons registered under this Part to pay a periodic fee to the Council of such amount, and at such time, as the rules may specify.

(4) No rules shall be made by a Council under this Part without the consent of the appropriate Minister.

PART V

THE CHILDREN'S COMMISSIONER FOR WALES

Children's
Commissioner for
Wales.

72.—(1) There shall be an office of the Children's Commissioner for Wales or Comisiynydd Plant Cymru.

(2) Schedule 2 shall have effect with respect to the Children's Commissioner for Wales (referred to in this Act as "the Commissioner").

Review and
monitoring of
arrangements.

73.—(1) The Commissioner may review, and monitor the operation of, arrangements falling within subsection (2), (3) or (4) for the purpose of ascertaining whether, and to what extent, the arrangements are effective in safeguarding and promoting the rights and welfare of children to whom this Part applies.

(2) The arrangements falling within this subsection are the arrangements made by the providers of regulated children's services in Wales, or by the Assembly, for dealing with complaints or representations in respect of such services made by or on behalf of children to whom this Part applies.

(3) The arrangements falling within this subsection are arrangements made by the providers of regulated children's services in Wales, or by the Assembly, for ensuring that proper action is taken in response to any disclosure of information which may tend to show—

(a) that a criminal offence has been committed;

(b) that a person has failed to comply with any legal obligation to which he is subject;

(c) that the health and safety of any person has been endangered; or

(d) that information tending to show that any matter falling within one of the preceding paragraphs has been deliberately concealed,

in the course of or in connection with the provision of such services.

(4) The arrangements falling within this subsection are arrangements made (whether by providers of regulated children's services in Wales, by the Assembly or by any other person) for making persons available—

(a) to represent the views and wishes of children to whom this Part applies; or

(b) to provide such children with advice and support of any prescribed kind.

(5) Regulations may confer power on the Commissioner to require prescribed persons to provide any information which the Commissioner considers it necessary or expedient to have for the purposes of his functions under this section.

Examination of
cases.

74.—(1) Regulations may make provision for the examination by the Commissioner of the cases of particular children to whom this Part applies.

(2) The regulations may include provision about—

(a) the types of case which may be examined;

(b) the circumstances in which an examination may be made;

(c) the procedure for conducting an examination, including provision about the representation of parties;

(d) the publication of reports following an examination.

(3) The regulations may make provision for—

(a) requiring persons to provide the Commissioner with information; or

(b) requiring persons who hold or are accountable for information to provide the Commissioner with explanations or other assistance,

for the purposes of an examination or for the purposes of determining whether any recommendation made in a report following an examination has been complied with.

(4) For the purposes mentioned in subsection (3), the Commissioner shall have the same powers as the High Court in respect of—

(a) the attendance and examination of witnesses (including the administration of oaths and affirmations and the examination of witnesses abroad); and

(b) the provision of information.

(5) No person shall be compelled for the purposes mentioned in subsection (3) to give any evidence or provide any information which he could not be compelled to give or provide in civil proceedings before the High Court.

(6) The regulations may make provision for the payment by the Commissioner of sums in respect of expenses or allowances to persons who attend or provide information for the purposes mentioned in subsection (3).

75.—(1) The Commissioner may certify an offence to the High Court where— Obstruction etc.

(a) a person, without lawful excuse, obstructs him or any member of his staff in the exercise of any of his functions under regulations made by virtue of section 73(5) or 74; or

(b) a person is guilty of any act or omission in relation to an examination under regulations made by virtue of section 74 which, if that examination were proceedings in the High Court, would constitute contempt of court.

(2) Where an offence is so certified the High Court may inquire into the matter; and after hearing—

(a) any witnesses who may be produced against or on behalf of the person charged with the offence; and

(b) any statement that may be offered in defence,

the High Court may deal with the person charged with the offence in any manner in which it could deal with him if he had committed the same offence in relation to the High Court.

76.—(1) Regulations may confer power on the Commissioner to assist a child to whom this Part applies— Further functions.

(a) in making a complaint or representation to or in respect of a provider of regulated children's services in Wales; or

(b) in any prescribed proceedings,

and in this subsection "proceedings" includes a procedure of any kind and any prospective proceedings.

(2) For the purposes of subsection (1), assistance includes—

(a) financial assistance; and

(b) arranging for representation, or the giving of advice or assistance, by any person,

and the regulations may provide for assistance to be given on conditions, including (in the case of financial assistance) conditions requiring repayment in circumstances specified in the regulations.

(3) The Commissioner may, in connection with his functions under this Part, give advice and information to any person.

(4) Regulations may, in connection with the Commissioner's functions under this Part, confer further functions on him.

(5) The regulations may, in particular, include provision about the making of reports on any matter connected with any of his functions.

(6) Apart from identifying any person investigated, a report by the Commissioner shall not—

(a) mention the name of any person; or

(b) include any particulars which, in the opinion of the Commissioner, are likely to identify any person and can be omitted without impairing the effectiveness of the report,

unless, after taking account of the public interest (as well as the interests of any person who made a complaint and other persons), the Commissioner considers it necessary for the report to mention his name or include such particulars.

(7) For the purposes of the law of defamation, the publication of any matter by the Commissioner in a report is absolutely privileged.

Restrictions.   **77.**—(1) This Part does not authorise the Commissioner to enquire into or report on any matter so far as it is the subject of legal proceedings before, or has been determined by, a court or tribunal.

(2) This Part does not authorise the Commissioner to exercise any function which by virtue of an enactment is also exercisable by a prescribed person.

Interpretation.   **78.**—(1) This Part applies to a child to or in respect of whom regulated children's services in Wales are provided.

(2) In this Part, "regulated children's services in Wales" means any of the following services for the time being provided in respect of children—

(a) services of a description provided by or in Part II undertakings, so far as provided in Wales;

(b) services provided by local authorities in Wales in the exercise of relevant adoption functions or relevant fostering functions;

(c) services of a description provided by persons registered under Part XA of the 1989 Act, so far as provided in Wales;

(d) accommodation provided by schools or by an institution within the further education sector (as defined in section 91 of the Further and Higher Education Act 1992), so far as provided in Wales.

1992 c. 13.

(3) For the purposes of this Part—

(a) in the case of the services mentioned in subsection (2)(a), the person who carries on the Part II undertaking is to be treated as the provider of the services;

(b) in the case of the services mentioned in subsection (2)(d), the relevant person (as defined in section 87 of the 1989 Act) is to be treated as the provider of the services.

(4) For the purposes of this section, an establishment or agency, and an undertaking of any other description, is a Part II undertaking if the provider of the services in question is for the time being required to be registered under that Part.

(5) Where the activities of an undertaking are carried on from two or more branches, each of those branches shall be treated as a separate undertaking for the purposes of this Part.

(6) Regulations may provide—

(a) for this Part to be treated as having applied to a child at any time before the commencement of this Part if regulated children's services in Wales were at that time provided to or in respect of him;

(b) for references in this Part to children to whom this Part applies to include references to persons who, at any prescribed time, were such children.

(7) In this Part—

"information" includes information recorded in any form;

"regulations" means regulations made by the Assembly.

(8) In this section, "relevant adoption functions" and "relevant fostering functions" have the same meanings as in Part III.

PART VI

CHILD MINDING AND DAY CARE

79.—(1) After Part X of the 1989 Act (child minding and day care for young children) there shall be inserted—

Amendment of Children Act 1989.

"PART XA

CHILD MINDING AND DAY CARE FOR CHILDREN IN ENGLAND AND WALES

Introductory

Child minders and day care providers.

79A.—(1) This section and section 79B apply for the purposes of this Part.

(2) "Act as a child minder" means (subject to the following subsections) look after one or more children under the age of eight on domestic premises for reward; and "child minding" shall be interpreted accordingly.

(3) A person who—

    (a) is the parent, or a relative, of a child;

    (b) has parental responsibility for a child;

    (c) is a local authority foster parent in relation to a child;

    (d) is a foster parent with whom a child has been placed by a voluntary organisation; or

    (e) fosters a child privately,

does not act as a child minder when looking after that child.

(4) Where a person—

    (a) looks after a child for the parents ("P1"), or

    (b) in addition to that work, looks after another child for different parents ("P2"),

and the work consists (in a case within paragraph (a)) of looking after the child wholly or mainly in P1's home or (in a case within paragraph (b)) of looking after the children wholly or mainly in P1's home or P2's home or both, the work is not to be treated as child minding.

(5) In subsection (4), "parent", in relation to a child, includes—

    (a) a person who is not a parent of the child but who has parental responsibility for the child;

    (b) a person who is a relative of the child.

(6) "Day care" means care provided at any time for children under the age of eight on premises other than domestic premises.

(7) This Part does not apply in relation to a person who acts as a child minder, or provides day care on any premises, unless the period, or the total of the periods, in any day which he spends looking after children or (as the case may be) during which the children are looked after on the premises exceeds two hours.

(8) In determining whether a person is required to register under this Part for child minding, any day on which he does not act as a child minder at any time between 2 am and 6 pm is to be disregarded.

Other definitions, etc.

79B.—(1) The registration authority in relation to England is Her Majesty's Chief Inspector of Schools in England (referred to in this Part as the Chief Inspector) and references to the Chief Inspector's area are references to England.

(2) The registration authority in relation to Wales is the National Assembly for Wales (referred to in this Act as "the Assembly").

(3) A person is qualified for registration for child minding if—

(a) he, and every other person looking after children on any premises on which he is or is likely to be child minding, is suitable to look after children under the age of eight;

(b) every person living or employed on the premises in question is suitable to be in regular contact with children under the age of eight;

(c) the premises in question are suitable to be used for looking after children under the age of eight, having regard to their condition and the condition and appropriateness of any equipment on the premises and to any other factor connected with the situation, construction or size of the premises; and

(d) he is complying with regulations under section 79C and with any conditions imposed by the registration authority.

(4) A person is qualified for registration for providing day care on particular premises if—

(a) every person looking after children on the premises is suitable to look after children under the age of eight;

(b) every person living or working on the premises is suitable to be in regular contact with children under the age of eight;

(c) the premises are suitable to be used for looking after children under the age of eight, having regard to their condition and the condition and appropriateness of any equipment on the premises and to any other factor connected with the situation, construction or size of the premises; and

(d) he is complying with regulations under section 79C and with any conditions imposed by the registration authority.

(5) For the purposes of subsection (4)(b) a person is not treated as working on the premises in question if—

(a) none of his work is done in the part of the premises in which children are looked after; or

(b) he does not work on the premises at times when children are looked after there.

(6) "Domestic premises" means any premises which are wholly or mainly used as a private dwelling and "premises" includes any area and any vehicle.

(7) "Regulations" means—

(a) in relation to England, regulations made by the Secretary of State;

(b) in relation to Wales, regulations made by the Assembly.

(8) "Tribunal" means the Tribunal established by section 9 of the Protection of Children Act 1999.

(9) Schedule 9A (which supplements the provisions of this Part) shall have effect.

Regulations

Regulations etc. governing child minders and day care providers.

79C.—(1) The Secretary of State may, after consulting the Chief Inspector and any other person he considers appropriate, make regulations governing the activities of registered persons who act as child minders, or provide day care, on premises in England.

(2) The Assembly may make regulations governing the activities of registered persons who act as child minders, or provide day care, on premises in Wales.

(3) The regulations under this section may deal with the following matters (among others)—

(a) the welfare and development of the children concerned;

(b) suitability to look after, or be in regular contact with, children under the age of eight;

(c) qualifications and training;

(d) the maximum number of children who may be looked after and the number of persons required to assist in looking after them;

(e) the maintenance, safety and suitability of premises and equipment;

(f) the keeping of records;

(g) the provision of information.

(4) In relation to activities on premises in England, the power to make regulations under this section may be exercised so as to confer powers or impose duties on the Chief Inspector in the exercise of his functions under this Part.

(5) In particular they may be exercised so as to require or authorise the Chief Inspector, in exercising those functions, to have regard to or meet factors, standards and other matters prescribed by or referred to in the regulations.

(6) If the regulations require any person (other than the registration authority) to have regard to or meet factors, standards and other matters prescribed by or referred to in the regulations, they may also provide for any allegation that the person has failed to do so to be taken into account—

(a) by the registration authority in the exercise of its functions under this Part, or

(b) in any proceedings under this Part.

(7) Regulations may provide—

(a) that a registered person who without reasonable excuse contravenes, or otherwise fails to comply with, any requirement of the regulations shall be guilty of an offence; and

(b) that a person guilty of the offence shall be liable on summary conviction to a fine not exceeding level 5 on the standard scale.

Registration

Requirement to register.

79D.—(1) No person shall—

(a) act as a child minder in England unless he is registered under this Part for child minding by the Chief Inspector; or

(b) act as a child minder in Wales unless he is registered under this Part for child minding by the Assembly.

(2) Where it appears to the registration authority that a person has contravened subsection (1), the authority may serve a notice ("an enforcement notice") on him.

(3) An enforcement notice shall have effect for a period of one year beginning with the date on which it is served.

(4) If a person in respect of whom an enforcement notice has effect contravenes subsection (1) without reasonable excuse (whether the contravention occurs in England or Wales), he shall be guilty of an offence.

(5) No person shall provide day care on any premises unless he is registered under this Part for providing day care on those premises by the registration authority.

(6) If any person contravenes subsection (5) without reasonable excuse, he shall be guilty of an offence.

(7) A person guilty of an offence under this section shall be liable on summary conviction to a fine not exceeding level 5 on the standard scale.

Applications for registration.

79E.—(1) A person who wishes to be registered under this Part shall make an application to the registration authority.

(2) The application shall—

(a) give prescribed information about prescribed matters;

(b) give any other information which the registration authority reasonably requires the applicant to give.

(3) Where a person provides, or proposes to provide, day care on different premises, he shall make a separate application in respect of each of them.

(4) Where the registration authority has sent the applicant notice under section 79L(1) of its intention to

refuse an application under this section, the application may not be withdrawn without the consent of the authority.

(5) A person who, in an application under this section, knowingly makes a statement which is false or misleading in a material particular shall be guilty of an offence and liable, on summary conviction, to a fine not exceeding level 5 on the standard scale.

Grant or refusal of registration.

79F.—(1) If, on an application by a person for registration for child minding—

    (a) the registration authority is of the opinion that the applicant is, and will continue to be, qualified for registration for child minding (so far as the conditions of section 79B(3) are applicable); and

    (b) the applicant pays the prescribed fee,

the authority shall grant the application; otherwise, it shall refuse it.

(2) If, on an application by any person for registration for providing day care on any premises—

    (a) the registration authority is of the opinion that the applicant is, and will continue to be, qualified for registration for providing day care on those premises (so far as the conditions of section 79B(4) are applicable); and

    (b) the applicant pays the prescribed fee,

the authority shall grant the application; otherwise, it shall refuse it.

(3) An application may, as well as being granted subject to any conditions the authority thinks necessary or expedient for the purpose of giving effect to regulations under section 79C, be granted subject to any other conditions the authority thinks fit to impose.

(4) The registration authority may as it thinks fit vary or remove any condition to which the registration is subject or impose a new condition.

(5) Any register kept by a registration authority of persons who act as child minders or provide day care shall be open to inspection by any person at all reasonable times.

(6) A registered person who without reasonable excuse contravenes, or otherwise fails to comply with, any condition imposed on his registration shall be guilty of an offence.

(7) A person guilty of an offence under subsection (6) shall be liable on summary conviction to a fine not exceeding level 5 on the standard scale.

Cancellation of registration.

79G.—(1) The registration authority may cancel the registration of any person if—

(a) in the case of a person registered for child minding, the authority is of the opinion that the person has ceased or will cease to be qualified for registration for child minding;

(b) in the case of a person registered for providing day care on any premises, the authority is of the opinion that the person has ceased or will cease to be qualified for registration for providing day care on those premises,

or if an annual fee which is due from the person has not been paid.

(2) Where a requirement to make any changes or additions to any services, equipment or premises has been imposed on a registered person under section 79F(3), his registration shall not be cancelled on the ground of any defect or insufficiency in the services, equipment or premises if—

(a) the time set for complying with the requirements has not expired; and

(b) it is shown that the defect or insufficiency is due to the changes or additions not having been made.

(3) Any cancellation under this section must be in writing.

Suspension of registration.

79H.—(1) Regulations may provide for the registration of any person for acting as a child minder or providing day care to be suspended for a prescribed period by the registration authority in prescribed circumstances.

(2) Any regulations made under this section shall include provision conferring on the person concerned a right of appeal to the Tribunal against suspension.

Resignation of registration.

79J.—(1) A person who is registered for acting as a child minder or providing day care may by notice in writing to the registration authority resign his registration.

(2) But a person may not give a notice under subsection (1)—

(a) if the registration authority has sent him a notice under section 79L(1) of its intention to cancel the registration, unless the authority has decided not to take that step; or

(b) if the registration authority has sent him a notice under section 79L(5) of its decision to cancel the registration and the time within which an appeal may be brought has not expired or, if an appeal has been brought, it has not been determined.

Protection of children in an emergency.

79K.—(1) If, in the case of any person registered for acting as a child minder or providing day care—

(a) the registration authority applies to a justice of the peace for an order—

(i) cancelling the registration;

(ii) varying or removing any condition to which the registration is subject; or

(iii) imposing a new condition; and

(b) it appears to the justice that a child who is being, or may be, looked after by that person, or (as the case may be) in accordance with the provision for day care made by that person, is suffering, or is likely to suffer, significant harm,

the justice may make the order.

(2) The cancellation, variation, removal or imposition shall have effect from the time when the order is made.

(3) An application under subsection (1) may be made without notice.

(4) An order under subsection (1) shall be made in writing.

(5) Where an order is made under this section, the registration authority shall serve on the registered person, as soon as is reasonably practicable after the making of the order—

(a) a copy of the order;

(b) a copy of any written statement of the authority's reasons for making the application for the order which supported that application; and

(c) notice of any right of appeal conferred by section 79M.

(6) Where an order has been so made, the registration authority shall, as soon as is reasonably practicable after the making of the order, notify the local authority in whose area the person concerned acts or acted as a child minder, or provides or provided day care, of the making of the order.

Notice of intention to take steps.

79L.—(1) Not less than 14 days before—

(a) refusing an application for registration;

(b) cancelling a registration;

(c) removing or varying any condition to which a registration is subject or imposing a new condition; or

(d) refusing to grant an application for the removal or variation of any condition to which a registration is subject,

the registration authority shall send to the applicant, or (as the case may be) registered person, notice in writing of its intention to take the step in question.

(2) Every such notice shall—

(a) give the authority's reasons for proposing to take the step; and

(b) inform the person concerned of his rights under this section.

(3) Where the recipient of such a notice informs the authority in writing of his desire to object to the step being taken, the authority shall afford him an opportunity to do so.

(4) Any objection made under subsection (3) may be made orally or in writing, by the recipient of the notice or a representative.

(5) If the authority, after giving the person concerned an opportunity to object to the step being taken, decides nevertheless to take it, it shall send him written notice of its decision.

(6) A step of a kind mentioned in subsection (1)(b) or (c) shall not take effect until the expiry of the time within which an appeal may be brought under section 79M or, where such an appeal is brought, before its determination.

(7) Subsection (6) does not prevent a step from taking effect before the expiry of the time within which an appeal may be brought under section 79M if the person concerned notifies the registration authority in writing that he does not intend to appeal.

Appeals.

79M.—(1) An appeal against—

(a) the taking of any step mentioned in section 79L(1); or

(b) an order under section 79K,

shall lie to the Tribunal.

(2) On an appeal, the Tribunal may—

(a) confirm the taking of the step or the making of the order or direct that it shall not have, or shall cease to have, effect; and

(b) impose, vary or cancel any condition.

Inspection: England

General functions of the Chief Inspector.

79N.—(1) The Chief Inspector has the general duty of keeping the Secretary of State informed about the quality and standards of child minding and day care provided by registered persons in England.

(2) When asked to do so by the Secretary of State, the Chief Inspector shall give advice or information to the Secretary of State about such matters relating to the provision of child minding or day care by registered persons in England as may be specified in the Secretary of State's request.

(3) The Chief Inspector may at any time give advice to the Secretary of State, either generally or in relation to provision by particular persons or on particular premises, on any matter connected with the provision of child minding or day care by registered persons in England.

(4) The Chief Inspector may secure the provision of training for persons who provide or assist in providing child minding or day care, or intend to do so.

(5) Regulations may confer further functions on the Chief Inspector relating to child minding and day care provided in England.

1996 c. 57.

(6) The annual reports of the Chief Inspector required by subsection (7)(a) of section 2 of the School Inspections Act 1996 to be made to the Secretary of State shall include an account of the exercise of the Chief Inspector's functions under this Part, and the power conferred by subsection (7)(b) of that section to make other reports to the Secretary of State includes a power to make reports with respect to matters which fall within the scope of his functions by virtue of this Part.

Early years child care inspectorate.

79P.—(1) The Chief Inspector shall establish and maintain a register of early years child care inspectors for England.

(2) The register may be combined with the register maintained for England under paragraph 8(1) of Schedule 26 to the School Standards and Framework Act 1998 (register of nursery education inspectors).

1998 c. 31.

(3) Paragraphs 8(2) to (9), 9(1) to (4), 10 and 11 of that Schedule shall apply in relation to the register of early years child care inspectors as they apply in relation to the register maintained for England under paragraph 8(1) of that Schedule, but with the modifications set out in subsection (4).

(4) In the provisions concerned—

(a) references to registered nursery education inspectors shall be read as references to registered early years child care inspectors;

(b) references to inspections under paragraph 6 of that Schedule shall be read as references to inspections under section 79Q (and references to the functions of a registered nursery education inspector under paragraph 6 shall be interpreted accordingly);

(c) references to the registration of a person under paragraph 6 of that Schedule shall be read as references to the registration of a person under subsection (1) (and references to applications made under paragraph 6 shall be interpreted accordingly); and

(d) in paragraph 10(2), for the words from "to a tribunal" to the end there shall be substituted "to the Tribunal established under section 9 of the Protection of Children Act 1999."

1999 c. 14.

(5) Registered early years child care inspectors are referred to below in this Part as registered inspectors.

Inspection of provision of child minding and day care in England.

79Q.—(1) The Chief Inspector may at any time require any registered person to provide him with any information connected with the person's activities as a child minder, or provision of day care, which the Chief Inspector considers it necessary to have for the purposes of his functions under this Part.

(2) The Chief Inspector shall secure that any child minding provided in England by a registered person is inspected by a registered inspector at prescribed intervals.

(3) The Chief Inspector shall secure that any day care provided by a registered person on any premises in England is inspected by a registered inspector at prescribed intervals.

(4) The Chief Inspector may comply with subsection (2) or (3) either by organising inspections or by making arrangements with others for them to organise inspections.

(5) In prescribing the intervals mentioned in subsection (2) or (3) the Secretary of State may make provision as to the period within which the first inspection of child minding or day care provided by any person or at any premises is to take place.

(6) A person conducting an inspection under this section shall report on the quality and standards of the child minding or day care provided.

(7) The Chief Inspector may arrange for an inspection conducted by a registered inspector under this section to be monitored by another registered inspector.

Reports of inspections.

79R.—(1) A person who has conducted an inspection under section 79Q shall report in writing on the matters inspected to the Chief Inspector within the prescribed period.

(2) The period mentioned in subsection (1) may, if the Chief Inspector considers it necessary, be extended by up to three months.

(3) Once the report of an inspection has been made to the Chief Inspector under subsection (1) he—

    (a) may send a copy of it to the Secretary of State, and shall do so without delay if the Secretary of State requests a copy;

    (b) shall send a copy of it, or of such parts of it as he considers appropriate, to any prescribed authorities or persons; and

    (c) may arrange for the report (or parts of it) to be further published in any manner he considers appropriate.

(4) Subsections (2) to (4) of section 42A of the School Inspections Act 1996 shall apply in relation to the publication of any report under subsection (3) as they

1996 c. 57.

apply in relation to the publication of a report under any of the provisions mentioned in subsection (2) of section 42A.

Inspection: Wales

General functions of the Assembly.

79S.—(1) The Assembly may secure the provision of training for persons who provide or assist in providing child minding or day care, or intend to do so.

(2) In relation to child minding and day care provided in Wales, the Assembly shall have any additional function specified in regulations made by the Assembly; but the regulations may only specify a function corresponding to a function which, by virtue of section 79N(5), is exercisable by the Chief Inspector in relation to child minding and day care provided in England.

Inspection: Wales.

79T.—(1) The Assembly may at any time require any registered person to provide it with any information connected with the person's activities as a child minder or provision of day care which the Assembly considers it necessary to have for the purposes of its functions under this Part.

(2) The Assembly may by regulations make provision—

(a) for the inspection of the quality and standards of child minding provided in Wales by registered persons and of day care provided by registered persons on premises in Wales;

(b) for the publication of reports of the inspections in such manner as the Assembly considers appropriate.

(3) The regulations may provide for the inspections to be organised by—

(a) the Assembly; or

(b) Her Majesty's Chief Inspector of Education and Training in Wales, or any other person, under arrangements made with the Assembly.

1996 c. 57.

(4) The regulations may provide for subsections (2) to (4) of section 42A of the School Inspections Act 1996 to apply with modifications in relation to the publication of reports under the regulations.

Supplementary

Rights of entry etc.

79U.—(1) An authorised inspector may at any reasonable time enter any premises in England or Wales on which child minding or day care is at any time provided.

(2) Where an authorised inspector has reasonable cause to believe that a child is being looked after on any premises in contravention of this Part, he may enter those premises at any reasonable time.

Care Standards Act 2000   c. **14**   51

PART VI

(3) An inspector entering premises under this section may—

(a) inspect the premises;

(b) inspect, and take copies of—

(i) any records kept by the person providing the child minding or day care; and

(ii) any other documents containing information relating to its provision;

(c) seize and remove any document or other material or thing found there which he has reasonable grounds to believe may be evidence of a failure to comply with any condition or requirement imposed by or under this Part;

(d) require any person to afford him such facilities and assistance with respect to matters within the person's control as are necessary to enable him to exercise his powers under this section;

(e) take measurements and photographs or make recordings;

(f) inspect any children being looked after there, and the arrangements made for their welfare;

(g) interview in private the person providing the child minding or day care; and

(h) interview in private any person looking after children, or living or working, there who consents to be interviewed.

(4) Section 42 of the School Inspections Act 1996 (inspection of computer records for purposes of Part I of that Act) shall apply for the purposes of subsection (3) as it applies for the purposes of Part I of that Act.

1996 c. 57.

(5) The registration authority may, in any case where it appears to the authority appropriate to do so, authorise a person who is not an authorised inspector to exercise any of the powers conferred by this section.

(6) A person exercising any power conferred by this section shall, if so required, produce some duly authenticated document showing his authority to do so.

(7) It shall be an offence wilfully to obstruct a person exercising any such power.

(8) Any person guilty of an offence under subsection (7) shall be liable on summary conviction to a fine not exceeding level 4 on the standard scale.

(9) In this section—

"authorised inspector" means a registered inspector or a person authorised by the Assembly or by any person with whom the Assembly has made arrangements under section 79T(3);

"documents" and "records" each include information recorded in any form.

Function of
local authorities.

79V. Each local authority shall, in accordance with regulations, secure the provision—

    (a) of information and advice about child minding and day care; and

    (b) of training for persons who provide or assist in providing child minding or day care.

Checks on suitability of persons working with children over the age of seven

Requirement for
certificate of
suitability.

79W.—(1) This section applies to any person not required to register under this Part who looks after, or provides care for, children and meets the following conditions.

References in this section to children are to those under the age of 15 or (in the case of disabled children) 17.

(2) The first condition is that the period, or the total of the periods, in any week which he spends looking after children or (as the case may be) during which the children are looked after exceeds five hours.

(3) The second condition is that he would be required to register under this Part (or, as the case may be, this Part if it were subject to prescribed modifications) if the children were under the age of eight.

(4) Regulations may require a person to whom this section applies to hold a certificate issued by the registration authority as to his suitability, and the suitability of each prescribed person, to look after children.

(5) The regulations may make provision about—

    (a) applications for certificates;

    (b) the matters to be taken into account by the registration authority in determining whether to issue certificates;

    (c) the information to be contained in certificates;

    (d) the period of their validity.

(6) The regulations may provide that a person to whom this section applies shall be guilty of an offence—

    (a) if he does not hold a certificate as required by the regulations; or

    (b) if, being a person who holds such a certificate, he fails to produce it when reasonably required to do so by a prescribed person.

(7) The regulations may provide that a person who, for the purpose of obtaining such a certificate, knowingly makes a statement which is false or misleading in a material particular shall be guilty of an offence.

(8) The regulations may provide that a person guilty of an offence under the regulations shall be liable on summary conviction to a fine not exceeding level 5 on the standard scale.

Time limit for proceedings

Time limit for proceedings.

79X. Proceedings for an offence under this Part or regulations made under it may be brought within a period of six months from the date on which evidence sufficient in the opinion of the prosecutor to warrant the proceedings came to his knowledge; but no such proceedings shall be brought by virtue of this section more than three years after the commission of the offence."

(2) Schedule 3 (which inserts a new Schedule 9A in the 1989 Act) shall have effect.

(3) The appropriate Minister may by order make a scheme for the transfer to the new employer of any eligible employee.

(4) In subsection (3)—

"eligible employee" means a person who is employed under a contract of employment with an old employer on work which would have continued but for the provisions of this section;

"new employer" means the registration authority (within the meaning of Part XA of the 1989 Act) and, in relation to Wales, includes Her Majesty's Chief Inspector of Education and Training in Wales;

"old employer" means a local authority.

(5) Part X of, and Schedule 9 to, the 1989 Act shall cease to extend to England and Wales.

PART VII

PROTECTION OF CHILDREN AND VULNERABLE ADULTS

Protection of vulnerable adults

80.—(1) Subsections (2) to (7) apply for the purposes of this Part.

Basic definitions.

(2) "Care worker" means—

    (a) an individual who is or has been employed in a position which is such as to enable him to have regular contact in the course of his duties with adults to whom accommodation is provided at a care home;

    (b) an individual who is or has been employed in a position which is such as to enable him to have regular contact in the course of his duties with adults to whom prescribed services are provided by an independent hospital, an independent clinic, an independent medical agency or a National Health Service body;

    (c) an individual who is or has been employed in a position which is concerned with the provision of personal care in their own homes for persons who by reason of illness, infirmity or disability are unable to provide it for themselves without assistance.

(3) "Care position", in relation to an individual, means a position such as is mentioned in subsection (2)(a), (b) or (c).

(4) "Employment" has the same meaning as in the Protection of Children Act 1999 (referred to in this Act as "the 1999 Act"); and references to an individual being employed shall be construed accordingly.

(5) "Supply worker"—

    (a) in relation to an employment agency, means an individual supplied by the agency for employment in a care position or for whom the agency has found employment in a care position;

    (b) in relation to an employment business, means an individual supplied by the business for employment in a care position.

(6) "Vulnerable adult" means—

    (a) an adult to whom accommodation and nursing or personal care are provided in a care home;

    (b) an adult to whom personal care is provided in their own home under arrangements made by a domiciliary care agency; or

    (c) an adult to whom prescribed services are provided by an independent hospital, independent clinic, independent medical agency or National Health Service body.

(7) The persons who provide care for vulnerable adults are—

    (a) any person who carries on a care home;

    (b) any person who carries on a domiciliary care agency;

    (c) any person who carries on an independent hospital, an independent clinic or an independent medical agency, which provides prescribed services; and

    (d) a National Health Service body which provides prescribed services.

(8) Regulations for the purposes of this section or section 91, 93 or 103 may only be made by the Secretary of State; and before making any regulations for the purposes of this section or section 93 or 103 the Secretary of State shall consult the Assembly.

Duty of Secretary of State to keep list.

81.—(1) The Secretary of State shall keep a list of individuals who are considered unsuitable to work with vulnerable adults.

(2) An individual shall not be included in the list except in accordance with this Part.

(3) The Secretary of State may at any time remove an individual from the list if he is satisfied that the individual should not have been included in it.

Persons who provide care for vulnerable adults: duty to refer.

82.—(1) A person who provides care for vulnerable adults ("the provider") shall refer a care worker to the Secretary of State if there is fulfilled—

    (a) any of the conditions mentioned in subsection (2); or

    (b) the condition mentioned in subsection (3).

(2) The conditions referred to in subsection (1)(a) are—

(a) that the provider has dismissed the worker on the grounds of misconduct (whether or not in the course of his employment) which harmed or placed at risk of harm a vulnerable adult;

(b) that the worker has resigned, retired or been made redundant in circumstances such that the provider would have dismissed him, or would have considered dismissing him, on such grounds if he had not resigned, retired or been made redundant;

(c) that the provider has, on such grounds, transferred the worker to a position which is not a care position;

(d) that the provider has, on such grounds, suspended the worker or provisionally transferred him to a position which is not a care position but has not yet decided whether to dismiss him or to confirm the transfer.

(3) The condition referred to in subsection (1)(b) is that—

(a) in circumstances not falling within subsection (2), the provider has dismissed the worker, he has resigned or retired or the provider has transferred him to a position which is not a care position;

(b) information not available to the provider at the time of the dismissal, resignation, retirement or transfer has since become available; and

(c) the provider has formed the opinion that, if that information had been available at that time and if (where applicable) the worker had not resigned or retired, the provider would have dismissed him, or would have considered dismissing him, on such grounds as are mentioned in subsection (2)(a).

(4) If it appears from the information submitted with a reference under subsection (1) that it may be appropriate for the worker to be included in the list kept under section 81, the Secretary of State shall—

(a) determine the reference in accordance with subsections (5) to (7); and

(b) pending that determination, provisionally include the worker in the list.

(5) The Secretary of State shall—

(a) invite observations from the worker on the information submitted with the reference and, if he thinks fit, on any observations submitted under paragraph (b); and

(b) invite observations from the provider on any observations on the information submitted with the reference and, if he thinks fit, on any other observations under paragraph (a).

(6) Where—

(a) the Secretary of State has considered the information submitted with the reference, any observations submitted to him and any other information which he considers relevant; and

(b) in the case of a reference under subsection (2)(d), the provider has dismissed the worker or, as the case may be, has confirmed his transfer on such grounds as are there mentioned,

the Secretary of State shall confirm the worker's inclusion in the list if subsection (7) applies; otherwise he shall remove him from the list.

(7) This subsection applies if the Secretary of State is of the opinion—

    (a) that the provider reasonably considered the worker to be guilty of misconduct (whether or not in the course of his employment) which harmed or placed at risk of harm a vulnerable adult; and

    (b) that the worker is unsuitable to work with vulnerable adults.

(8) The reference in subsection (6)(b) to the provider dismissing the worker on such grounds as are mentioned in subsection (2)(d) includes—

    (a) a reference to his resigning, retiring or being made redundant in circumstances such that the provider would have dismissed him, or would have considered dismissing him, on such grounds if he had not resigned, retired or been made redundant; and

    (b) a reference to the provider transferring him, on such grounds, to a position which is not a care position.

(9) This section does not apply where—

    (a) the provider carries on a domiciliary care agency, or an independent medical agency, which is or includes an employment agency or an employment business; and

    (b) the worker in question is a supply worker in relation to him.

(10) Nothing in this section shall require a person who provides care for vulnerable adults to refer a worker to the Secretary of State in any case where the dismissal, resignation, retirement, transfer or suspension took place or, as the case may be, the opinion was formed before the commencement of this section.

Employment agencies and businesses: duty to refer.

83.—(1) A person who carries on an employment agency or an employment business ("the provider") shall refer a supply worker to the Secretary of State if there is fulfilled—

    (a) in the case of an employment agency, any of the conditions mentioned in subsection (2); or

    (b) in the case of an employment business, any of the conditions mentioned in subsection (3).

(2) The conditions referred to in subsection (1)(a) are—

    (a) that the provider has decided not to do any further business with the worker on grounds of misconduct (whether or not in the course of his employment) which harmed or placed at risk of harm a vulnerable adult;

    (b) that the provider has decided on such grounds not to find the worker further employment, or supply him for further employment, in a care position.

(3) The conditions mentioned in subsection (1)(b) are—

    (a) that the provider has dismissed the worker on the grounds of misconduct (whether or not in the course of his employment) which harmed or placed at risk of harm a vulnerable adult;

    (b) that the worker has resigned or retired in circumstances such that the provider would have dismissed him, or would have considered dismissing him, on such grounds if he had not resigned or retired;

    (c) that the provider has, on such grounds, decided not to supply the worker for further employment in a care position.

(4) If it appears from the information submitted with a reference under subsection (1) that it may be appropriate for the worker to be included in the list kept under section 81, the Secretary of State shall—

    (a) determine the reference in accordance with subsections (5) to (7); and

    (b) pending that determination, provisionally include the worker in the list.

(5) The Secretary of State shall—

    (a) invite observations from the worker on the information submitted with the reference and, if he thinks fit, on any observations submitted under paragraph (b); and

    (b) invite observations from the provider on any observations on the information submitted with the reference and, if he thinks fit, on any other observations under paragraph (a).

(6) Where the Secretary of State has considered the information submitted with the reference, any observations submitted to him and any other information which he considers relevant, the Secretary of State shall confirm the worker's inclusion in the list if subsection (7) applies; otherwise he shall remove him from the list.

(7) This subsection applies if the Secretary of State is of the opinion—

    (a) that the provider reasonably considered the worker to be guilty of misconduct (whether or not in the course of his employment) which harmed or placed at risk of harm a vulnerable adult; and

    (b) that the worker is unsuitable to work with vulnerable adults.

(8) Nothing in this section shall require a person who provides care for vulnerable adults to refer a worker to the Secretary of State in any case where the dismissal, resignation or retirement took place or, as the case may be, the decision was made before the commencement of this section.

84.—(1) The registration authority may refer a care worker to the Secretary of State if— Power of registration authority to refer.

    (a) on the basis of evidence obtained by it in the exercise of its functions under Part II of this Act, the authority considers that the worker has been guilty of misconduct (whether or not in the course of his employment) which harmed or placed at risk of harm a vulnerable adult; and

    (b) the worker has not been referred to the Secretary of State under section 82 or 83 in respect of the misconduct.

(2) Section 82(4) to (7) shall apply in relation to a reference made by the registration authority under subsection (1) as it applies in relation to a reference made by a person under section 82(1).

(3) The reference in subsection (1) to misconduct is to misconduct which occurred after the commencement of this section.

85.—(1) Subsection (2) applies where— Individuals named in the findings of certain inquiries.

    (a) a relevant inquiry has been held;

    (b) the report of the person who held the inquiry names an individual who is or has been employed in a care position; and

    (c) it appears to the Secretary of State from the report—

     (i) that the person who held the inquiry found that the individual was guilty of relevant misconduct; and

     (ii) that the individual is unsuitable to work with vulnerable adults.

(2) The Secretary of State—

 (a) may provisionally include the individual in the list kept under section 81; and

 (b) if he does so, shall determine in accordance with subsections (3) to (5) whether the individual's inclusion in the list should be confirmed.

(3) The Secretary of State shall—

 (a) invite observations from the individual on the report, so far as relating to him, and, if the Secretary of State thinks fit, on any observations submitted under paragraph (b); and

 (b) invite observations from the relevant employer on any observations on the report and, if the Secretary of State thinks fit, on any other observations under paragraph (a).

(4) Where the Secretary of State has considered the report, any observations submitted to him and any other information which he considers relevant, he shall confirm that individual's inclusion in the list if subsection (5) applies; otherwise he shall remove him from the list.

(5) This subsection applies if the Secretary of State is of the opinion—

 (a) that the person who held the inquiry reasonably considered the individual to be guilty of relevant misconduct; and

 (b) that the individual is unsuitable to work with vulnerable adults.

(6) In this section—

"relevant employer" means the person who, at the time mentioned in the definition of "relevant misconduct" below, employed the individual in a care position;

"relevant misconduct" means misconduct which harmed or placed at risk of harm a vulnerable adult and was committed (whether or not in the course of his employment) at a time when the individual was employed in a care position.

(7) In this section "relevant inquiry" means any of the following—

 (a) an inquiry held under—

  (i) section 10;

  (ii) section 35 of the Government of Wales Act 1998;

  (iii) section 81 of the 1989 Act;

  (iv) section 84 of the National Health Service Act 1977;

  (v) section 7C of the Local Authority Social Services Act 1970;

 (b) an inquiry to which the Tribunals of Inquiry (Evidence) Act 1921 applies;

 (c) any other inquiry or hearing designated for the purposes of this section by an order made by the Secretary of State.

(8) Before making an order under subsection (7) the Secretary of State shall consult the Assembly.

1998 c. 38.

1977 c. 49.

1970 c. 42.

1921 c. 7.

86.—(1) An individual who is included (otherwise than provisionally) in the list kept by the Secretary of State under section 81 may appeal to the Tribunal against—

(a) the decision to include him in the list; or

(b) with the leave of the Tribunal, any decision of the Secretary of State not to remove him from the list under section 81(3).

(2) Subject to subsection (5), an individual who has been provisionally included for a period of more than nine months in the list kept by the Secretary of State under section 81 may, with the leave of the Tribunal, have the issue of his inclusion in the list determined by the Tribunal instead of by the Secretary of State.

(3) If on an appeal or determination under this section the Tribunal is not satisfied of either of the following, namely—

(a) that the individual was guilty of misconduct (whether or not in the course of his duties) which harmed or placed at risk of harm a vulnerable adult; and

(b) that the individual is unsuitable to work with vulnerable adults,

the Tribunal shall allow the appeal or determine the issue in the individual's favour and (in either case) direct his removal from the list; otherwise it shall dismiss the appeal or direct the individual's inclusion in the list.

(4) Where an individual has been convicted of an offence involving misconduct (whether or not in the course of his employment) which harmed or placed at risk of harm a vulnerable adult, no finding of fact on which the conviction must be taken to have been based shall be challenged on an appeal or determination under this section.

(5) Where the misconduct of which the individual is alleged to have been guilty is the subject of any civil or criminal proceedings, an application for leave under subsection (2) may not be made before the end of the period of six months immediately following the final determination of the proceedings.

(6) For the purposes of subsection (5), proceedings are finally determined when—

(a) the proceedings are terminated without a decision being made;

(b) a decision is made against which no appeal lies;

(c) in a case where an appeal lies with leave against a decision, the time limited for applications for leave expires without leave being granted; or

(d) in a case where leave to appeal against a decision is granted or is not required, the time limited for appeal expires without an appeal being brought.

87.—(1) Subject to section 88, an individual who is included in the list kept by the Secretary of State under section 81 may make an application to the Tribunal under this section.

(2) On an application under this section the Tribunal shall determine whether or not the individual should continue to be included in the list.

(3) If the Tribunal is satisfied that the individual is no longer unsuitable to work with vulnerable adults it shall direct his removal from the list; otherwise it shall dismiss the application.

Conditions for application under section 87.

88.—(1) An individual may only make an application under section 87 with the leave of the Tribunal.

(2) An application for leave under this section may not be made unless the appropriate conditions are satisfied in the individual's case.

(3) In the case of an individual who was a child when he was included (otherwise than provisionally) in the list, the appropriate conditions are satisfied if—

(a) he has been so included for a continuous period of at least five years; and

(b) in the period of five years ending with the time when he makes the application under this section, he has made no other such application.

(4) In the case of any other individual, the appropriate conditions are satisfied if—

(a) he has been included (otherwise than provisionally) in the list for a continuous period of at least ten years; and

(b) in the period of ten years ending with the time when he makes the application under this section, he has made no other such application.

(5) The Tribunal shall not grant an application under this section unless it considers—

(a) that the individual's circumstances have changed since he was included (otherwise than provisionally) in the list, or, as the case may be, since he last made an application under this section; and

(b) that the change is such that leave should be granted.

Effect of inclusion in list.

89.—(1) Where a person who provides care to vulnerable adults proposes to offer an individual employment in a care position that person—

(a) shall ascertain whether the individual is included in the list kept under section 81; and

(b) if he is included in that list, shall not offer him employment in such a position.

(2) Where a person who provides care to vulnerable adults discovers that an individual employed by him in a care position is included in that list, he shall cease to employ him in a care position.

For the purposes of this subsection an individual is not employed in a care position if he has been suspended or provisionally transferred to a position which is not a care position.

(3) Where a person who provides care to vulnerable adults ("the provider") proposes to offer employment in a care position to an individual who has been supplied by a person who carries on an employment agency or employment business, there is a sufficient compliance with subsection (1) if the provider—

    (a) satisfies himself that, on a date within the last 12 months, the other person ascertained whether the individual was included in the list kept under section 81;

    (b) obtains written confirmation of the facts as ascertained by that person; and

    (c) if the individual was included in the list on that date, does not offer him employment in a care position.

(4) It is immaterial for the purposes of subsection (1) or (3) whether the individual is already employed by the provider.

(5) An individual who is included (otherwise than provisionally) in the list kept by the Secretary of State under section 81 shall be guilty of an offence if he knowingly applies for, offers to do, accepts or does any work in a care position.

(6) It shall be a defence for an individual charged with an offence under subsection (5) to prove that he did not know, and could not reasonably be expected to know, that he was so included in that list.

(7) An individual who is guilty of an offence under this section shall be liable—

    (a) on summary conviction, to imprisonment for a term not exceeding six months, or to a fine not exceeding the statutory maximum, or to both;

    (b) on conviction on indictment, to imprisonment for a term not exceeding five years, or to a fine, or to both.

90.—(1) After subsection (3B) of section 113 of the Police Act 1997 (criminal record certificates) there shall be inserted—

Searches of list under Part V of Police Act 1997.
1997 c. 50.

"(3C) If an application under this section is accompanied by a statement by the registered person that the certificate is required for the purpose of considering the applicant's suitability to be employed, supplied to work, found work or given work in a position (whether paid or unpaid) within subsection (3D), the criminal record certificate shall also state—

    (a) whether the applicant is included in the list kept under section 81 of the Care Standards Act 2000; and

    (b) if he is included in that list, such details of his inclusion as may be prescribed.

(3D) A position is within this subsection if it is—

    (a) a care position within the meaning of Part VII of the Care Standards Act 2000; or

    (b) a position of such other description as may be prescribed."

(2) After subsection (6A) of section 115 of that Act (enhanced criminal record certificates) there shall be inserted—

"(6B) If an application under this section is accompanied by a statement by the registered person that the certificate is required for the purpose of considering the applicant's suitability to be employed, supplied to work, found work or given work in a position (whether paid or unpaid) falling within subsection (3D) of section 113, the enhanced criminal record certificate shall also state—

(a) whether the applicant is included in the list kept under section 81 of the Care Standards Act 2000; and

(b) if he is included in that list, such details of his inclusion as may be prescribed."

Access to list before commencement of section 90.

91.—(1) In relation to any time before the commencement of section 90, any person seeking to ascertain whether a relevant individual is included in the list kept under section 81 shall be entitled to that information on making application for the purpose to the Secretary of State.

(2) For the purposes of subsection (1) a relevant individual is—

(a) an individual to whom the person proposes to offer employment in a care position;

(b) an individual for whom the person proposes to find employment, or whom he proposes to supply for employment, in a care position; or

(c) an individual of a prescribed description who does not fall within paragraph (a) or (b).

Persons referred for inclusion in list under Protection of Children Act 1999.

92.—(1) Section 2(4) to (7) of the 1999 Act (referrals for inclusion in list of individuals who are considered unsuitable to work with children) shall, in the case of any reference under section 2, 2A or 2D of that Act, apply in relation to the list kept under section 81 as they apply in relation to the list kept under section 1 of that Act, but as if the reference in subsection (7)(b) to children were a reference to vulnerable adults.

(2) Section 2B of the 1999 Act shall apply in relation to the list kept under section 81 as it applies in relation to the list kept under section 1 of that Act, but as if the references in subsections (1)(c)(ii) and (5)(b) to children were references to vulnerable adults.

(3) But the Secretary of State may not by virtue of subsection (1) or (2) provisionally include an individual in the list kept under section 81, or confirm his inclusion in that list, unless he provisionally includes him in the list kept under section 1 of the 1999 Act or, as the case requires, confirms his inclusion in that list.

(4) Where an individual has by virtue of subsection (1) or (2) been included in the list kept under section 81, section 86 shall apply to him as if the references in subsections (3)(a) and (4) to a vulnerable adult were references to a child.

Power to extend Part VII.

93.—(1) The Secretary of State may by regulations—

(a) add to the list in section 80(7) any prescribed persons to whom subsection (2) applies;

(b) amend the definitions of "care worker", "care position" and "vulnerable adult" accordingly.

(2) This subsection applies to—

(a) local authorities providing services to adults in the exercise of their social services functions;

(b) persons who provide to adults services which are similar to services which—

(i) may or must be so provided by local authorities; or

(ii) may or must be provided by National Health Service bodies.

(3) In its application by virtue of subsection (1), this Part shall have effect—

(a) if the regulations so provide, as if "may" were substituted for "shall" in sections 82(1) and 83(1), and section 89 were omitted;

(b) with such other modifications as may be specified in the regulations.

The list kept under section 1 of the 1999 Act

94.—(1) In subsection (9) of section 2 of the 1999 Act (inclusion on reference to Secretary of State in list of individuals who are considered unsuitable to work with children)—

Employment agencies and businesses.

(a) for "This section" there shall be substituted "Subsections (1) to (8) and (10) of this section"; and

(b) for the words from "(a)" to "harm" there shall be substituted—

"(a) in subsection (1), for the words from "there is" to the end there were substituted the following paragraphs—

"(a) the organisation has decided not to do any further business with the individual on the grounds of misconduct (whether or not in the course of his employment) which harmed a child or placed a child at risk of harm; or

(b) the organisation has decided on such grounds not to find the individual further employment, or supply him for further employment, in a child care position;"""

(2) After subsection (9) of that section there shall be inserted—

"(9A) Subsections (1) to (8) and (10) of this section shall have effect in relation to an organisation which carries on an employment business as if—

(a) in subsection (1)—

(i) for the words from "who" to "position" there were substituted the words "who has been supplied by the organisation for employment in a child care position"; and

(ii) paragraph (b) and the word "or" preceding it were omitted;

(b) for subsection (2)(c) and (d) there were substituted the following paragraph—

"(c) that the organisation has, on such grounds, decided not to supply the individual for further employment in a child care position." and

(c) subsections (3), (6)(b) and (8) were omitted."

95.—(1) After section 2 of the 1999 Act there is inserted—

Inclusion in 1999 Act list on reference by certain authorities.

"Power of certain authorities to refer individuals for inclusion in list.

2A.—(1) A person to whom this section applies may refer to the Secretary of State an individual who is or has been employed in a child care position if—

(a) on the basis of evidence obtained by him in the exercise of his functions under Part II of the

Care Standards Act 2000 or Part XA of the Children Act 1989, the person considers that the individual has been guilty of misconduct (whether or not in the course of his employment) which harmed a child or placed a child at risk of harm; and

(b) the individual has not been referred to the Secretary of State under section 1 above in respect of the misconduct.

(2) The persons to whom this section applies are—

(a) the National Care Standards Commission;

(b) the National Assembly for Wales; and

(c) Her Majesty's Chief Inspector of Schools in England.

(3) Section 2(4) to (7) above shall apply in relation to a reference made by a person under subsection (1) above as it applies in relation to a reference made by an organisation under section 2(1) above.

(4) The reference in subsection (1) above to misconduct is to misconduct which occurred after the commencement of this section."

(2) In section 1(2)(a) of that Act (duty of Secretary of State to keep list), after "2" there is inserted "or 2A".

(3) For the sidenote to section 2 of that Act there is substituted "Inclusion in list on reference following disciplinary action etc.".

Inclusion in 1999 Act list of individuals named in findings of certain inquiries.

96.—(1) After section 2A of the 1999 Act (inserted by section 95) there is inserted—

"Individuals named in the findings of certain inquiries.

2B.—(1) Subsection (2) applies where—

(a) a relevant inquiry has been held;

(b) the report of the person who held the inquiry names an individual who is or has been employed in a child care position; and

(c) it appears to the Secretary of State from the report—

(i) that the person who held the inquiry found that the individual was guilty of relevant misconduct; and

(ii) that the individual is unsuitable to work with children.

(2) The Secretary of State—

(a) may provisionally include the individual in the list kept under section 1 above; and

(b) if he does so, shall determine in accordance with subsections (3) to (5) below whether the individual's inclusion in the list should be confirmed.

(3) The Secretary of State shall—

(a) invite observations from the individual on the report, so far as relating to him, and, if the Secretary of State thinks fit, on any observations submitted under paragraph (b) below; and

(b) invite observations from the relevant employer on any observations on the report and, if the Secretary of State thinks fit, on any other observations under paragraph (a) above.

(4) Where the Secretary of State has considered the report, any observations submitted to him and any other information which he considers relevant, he shall confirm that individual's inclusion in the list if subsection (5) below applies; otherwise he shall remove him from the list.

(5) This subsection applies if the Secretary of State is of the opinion—

(a) that the person who held the inquiry reasonably considered the individual to be guilty of relevant misconduct; and

(b) that the individual is unsuitable to work with children.

(6) In this section—

"relevant employer" means the person who, at the time referred to in the definition of "relevant misconduct" below, employed the individual in a child care position;

"relevant misconduct" means misconduct which harmed a child or placed a child at risk of harm and was committed (whether or not in the course of his employment) at a time when the individual was employed in a child care position.

(7) In this section "relevant inquiry" means any of the following—

(a) an inquiry held under—

(i) section 10 of the Care Standards Act 2000;

(ii) section 35 of the Government of Wales Act 1998; 1998 c. 38.

(iii) section 81 of the Children Act 1989; 1989 c. 41.

(iv) section 84 of the National Health Service Act 1977; 1977 c. 49.

(v) section 7C of the Local Authority Social Services Act 1970; 1970 c. 42.

(b) an inquiry to which the Tribunals of Inquiry (Evidence) Act 1921 applies; 1921 c. 7.

(c) any other inquiry or hearing designated for the purposes of this section by an order made by the Secretary of State.

(8) An order under subsection (7) above shall be made by statutory instrument which shall be subject to annulment in pursuance of a resolution of either House of Parliament.

(9) Before making an order under subsection (7) above the Secretary of State shall consult the National Assembly for Wales."

(2) In section 1(2) of that Act (duty of Secretary of State to keep list), before the "or" preceding paragraph (b) there shall be inserted—

"(aa) he has been included in the list under section 2B below;".

Inclusion in 1999 Act list on reference under this Part.

97.—(1) After section 2B of the 1999 Act (inserted by section 95) there shall be inserted—

"Inclusion in list on reference under Part VII of Care Standards Act 2000.

2C.—(1) Section 82(4) to (7) of the Care Standards Act 2000 (persons who provide care for vulnerable adults: duty to refer) shall, in the case of any reference under subsection (1) of that section or section 84 of that Act, apply in relation to the list kept under section 1 above as it applies in relation to the list kept under section 81 of that Act, but as if the reference in subsection (7)(b) to vulnerable adults were a reference to children.

(2) Section 83(4) to (7) of that Act (employment agencies and businesses: duty to refer) shall, in the case of any reference under subsection (1) of that section, apply in relation to the list kept under section 1 above as it applies in relation to the list kept under section 81 of that Act, but as if the reference in subsection (7)(b) to vulnerable adults were a reference to children.

(3) Section 85 of that Act (individuals named in the findings of certain inquiries) shall apply in relation to the list kept under section 1 above as it applies in relation to the list kept under section 81 of that Act, but as if the references in subsections (1)(c)(ii) and (5)(b) to vulnerable adults were references to children.

(4) But the Secretary of State may not by virtue of this section provisionally include an individual in the list kept under section 1 above, or confirm his inclusion in that list, unless he provisionally includes him in the list kept under section 81 of that Act or, as the case requires, confirms his inclusion in that list.

(5) Where an individual has by virtue of this section been included in the list kept under section 1 above, section 4 below shall apply to him as if the references in subsections (3)(a) and (4) to a child were references to a vulnerable adult."

(2) In section 1(2)(a) of the 1999 Act (individuals who may be included on list), after "below" there shall be inserted "or Part VII of the Care Standards Act 2000".

Individuals providing care funded by direct payments.

98.—(1) After section 2C of the 1999 Act (inserted by section 97) there is inserted—

"Local authorities proposing to make direct payments in respect of services.

2D.—(1) A local authority may refer a relevant individual to the Secretary of State where, as a result of enquiries made, or caused to be made, by it under section 47 of the Children Act 1989, the authority considers that the individual has been guilty of misconduct (whether or not in the course of his employment) which harmed a child or placed a child at risk of harm.

1989 c. 41.

(2) Section 2(4) to (7) above shall apply in relation to a reference made by a local authority under subsection (1) above as it applies in relation to a reference made by an organisation under section 2(1) above.

(3) In this section—

> "funded care" means care in respect of a person's securing the provision of which the authority has made a payment under section 17A of the Children Act 1989 (direct payments);

> "relevant individual" means an individual who is or has been employed to provide funded care to a child.

(4) The reference in subsection (1) above to misconduct is to misconduct which occurred after the commencement of this section."

(2) In section 7 of that Act (effect of inclusion in certain statutory lists), after subsection (1) there shall be inserted—

"(1A) Where—

(a) a person ("the recipient") employs, or proposes to employ, an individual to provide care for a child; and

(b) a local authority proposes to make a payment to the recipient under section 17A of the Children Act 1989 (direct payments) in respect of his securing the provision of the care,

the authority shall, if the recipient asks it to do so, ascertain whether the individual is included in any of the lists mentioned in subsection (1) above."

(3) After subsection (2) of that section there shall be inserted—

"(2A) Where a local authority is required under subsection (1A) above to ascertain whether an individual who has been supplied as mentioned in subsection (2) above is included in any of the lists there mentioned, there is sufficient compliance with subsection (1A) above if the authority—

(a) satisfies itself that, on a date within the last 12 months, the organisation which supplied the individual ascertained whether he was included in any of those lists; and

(b) obtains written confirmation of the facts as ascertained by the organisation."

(4) In section 1(2)(a) of that Act (duty of Secretary of State to keep list), after "or 2A" there is inserted "or 2D".

PART VII
Transfer from
Consultancy
Service Index of
individuals named
in past inquiries.

99.—(1) Section 3 of the 1999 Act (inclusion in list on transfer from Consultancy Service Index) shall be amended as follows.

(2) In subsection (1), for "This section" there shall be substituted "Subsections (2) and (3) below" and in paragraph (a), for "this section" there shall be substituted "section 1 above".

(3) After subsection (3) there shall be inserted—

"(4) Subsections (5) and (6) below apply where—

(a) a relevant inquiry has been held;

(b) the report of the person who held the inquiry names an individual who is or has been employed in a child care position;

(c) it appears to the Secretary of State from the report—

(i) that the person who held the inquiry found that the individual was guilty of relevant misconduct; and

(ii) that the individual is unsuitable to work with children; and

(d) the individual is included in the Consultancy Service Index (otherwise than provisionally) immediately before the commencement of section 1 above.

(5) The Secretary of State shall—

(a) invite observations from the individual on the report, so far as relating to him, and, if the Secretary of State thinks fit, on any observations submitted under paragraph (b) below; and

(b) invite observations from the relevant employer on any observations on the report and, if the Secretary of State thinks fit, on any other observations under paragraph (a) above.

(6) The Secretary of State shall include the individual in the list kept by him under section 1 above if, after he has considered the report, any observations submitted to him and any other information which he considers relevant, he is of the opinion—

(a) that the person who held the inquiry reasonably considered the individual to be guilty of relevant misconduct; and

(b) that the individual is unsuitable to work with children.

(7) In this section—

"relevant employer", in relation to an individual named in the report of a relevant inquiry, means the person who, at the time referred to in the definition of "relevant misconduct" below, employed the individual in a child care position;

"relevant inquiry" has the same meaning as in section 2B above;

"relevant misconduct" means misconduct which harmed a child or placed a child at risk of harm and was committed (whether or not in the course of his employment) at a time when the individual was employed in a child care position."

Restrictions on working with children in independent schools

100.—(1) In subsection (1) of section 469 (notice of complaint) of the Education Act 1996, for paragraph (d) there shall be substituted—

Additional ground of complaint.
1996 c. 56.

"(d) the proprietor of the school or any teacher or other employee employed in the school—

(i) is unsuitable to work with children; or

(ii) is for any other reason not a proper person to be the proprietor of an independent school or (as the case may be) to be a teacher or other employee in any school;".

(2) In subsection (2) of section 470 of that Act (determination of complaint by an Independent Schools Tribunal), for paragraph (f) there shall be substituted—

"(f) if satisfied that any person alleged by the notice of complaint to be a person who—

(i) is unsuitable to work with children; or

(ii) is for any other reason not a proper person to be the proprietor of an independent school or to be a teacher or other employee in any school,

is in fact such a person, by order disqualify that person from being the proprietor of any independent school or (as the case may be) from being a teacher or other employee in any school."

101.—(1) Section 7 of the 1999 Act (effect of inclusion in either list) shall be amended as follows.

Effect of inclusion in 1996 Act list.

(2) For subsection (1) there shall be substituted—

"(1) Where a child care organisation proposes to offer an individual employment in a child care position, the organisation—

(a) shall ascertain whether the individual is included in—

(i) the list kept under section 1 above;

(ii) the list kept for the purposes of regulations made under section 218(6) of the 1988 Act ("the 1988 Act list"); or

(iii) any list kept by the Secretary of State or the National Assembly for Wales of persons disqualified under section 470 or 471 of the Education Act 1996 ("the 1996 Act list"); and

(b) if he is included in any of those lists, shall not offer him employment in such a position."

(3) In subsection (2)—

(a) in paragraph (a), for the words from "the list" to the end there shall be substituted "any of the lists mentioned in subsection (1) above"; and

(b) in paragraph (c), for "either list" there shall be substituted "any of those lists".

(4) For subsection (4) there shall be substituted—

"(4) In this section—

(a) any reference to inclusion in the 1988 Act list is a reference to inclusion in that list on the grounds mentioned in section 218(6ZA)(c) of the 1988 Act; and

(b) any reference to inclusion in the 1996 Act list is a reference to inclusion in that list as a person disqualified on the grounds mentioned in section 469(1)(d)(i) of the Education Act 1996."

1996 c. 56.

Searches of 1996 Act list.

1997 c. 50.

1999 c. 14.

1988 c. 40.

102.—(1) In subsection (3A) of section 113 of the Police Act 1997 (criminal record certificates), for the words from "in the list" to the end there shall be substituted "in—

> (i) the list kept under section 1 of the Protection of Children Act 1999;

> (ii) the list kept for the purposes of regulations made under section 218(6) of the Education Reform Act 1988 ("the 1988 Act list"); or

> (iii) any list kept by the Secretary of State or the National Assembly for Wales of persons disqualified under section 470 or 471 of the Education Act 1996 ("the 1996 Act list"); and

(b) if he is included in any of those lists, such details of his inclusion as may be prescribed, including—

> (i) in the case of the 1988 Act list, the grounds on which he is so included; or

> (ii) in the case of the 1996 Act list, the grounds on which he was disqualified under section 470 or 471."

(2) In subsection (6A) of section 115 of that Act (enhanced criminal record certificates), for the words from "in the list" to the end there shall be substituted "in—

> (i) the list kept under section 1 of the Protection of Children Act 1999;

> (ii) the list kept for the purposes of regulations made under section 218(6) of the Education Reform Act 1988 ("the 1988 Act list"); or

> (iii) any list kept by the Secretary of State or the National Assembly for Wales of persons disqualified under section 470 or 471 of the Education Act 1996 ("the 1996 Act list"); and

(b) if he is included in any of those lists, such details of his inclusion as may be prescribed, including—

> (i) in the case of the 1988 Act list, the grounds on which he is so included; or

> (ii) in the case of the 1996 Act list, the grounds on which he was disqualified under section 470 or 471."

General

Temporary provision for access to lists.

103.—(1) Any person seeking to ascertain whether a relevant individual is included in—

(a) the list kept under section 1 of the 1999 Act;

(b) the list kept for the purposes of regulations made under section 218(6) of the Education Reform Act 1988; or

(c) any list kept by the Secretary of State or the Assembly of persons disqualified under section 470 or 471 of the Education Act 1996,   1996 c. 56.

shall be entitled to that information on making, before the relevant commencement, an application for the purpose to the Secretary of State.

(2) In this section "relevant individual" means—

   (a) in relation to a person who carries on an employment agency, an individual with whom he proposes to do business or an individual of any other prescribed description;

   (b) in relation to any other person, an individual to whom he proposes to offer, or whom he proposes to supply for employment in, a child care position or an individual of any other prescribed description.

(3) The relevant commencement is—

   (a) for applications relating to the list mentioned in subsection (1)(a) or (b), the commencement of section 8 of the 1999 Act; and

   (b) for applications relating to the list mentioned in subsection (1)(c), the commencement of section 102.

(4) Paragraphs (b) and (c) of subsection (1) are without prejudice to any right conferred otherwise than by virtue of those provisions.

104.—(1) The Police Act 1997 shall be amended as follows.   Suitability to adopt a child: searches of lists.

(2) In section 113 (criminal record certificates)—   1997 c. 50.

   (a) in subsection (3A), after "(3B)," there shall be inserted "or his suitability to adopt a child,"; and

   (b) after subsection (3D) (inserted by section 90) there shall be inserted—

"(3E) The references in subsections (3A) and (3C) to suitability to be employed, supplied to work, found work or given work in a position falling within subsection (3B) or (3D) include references to suitability to be registered—

   (a) under Part II of the Care Standards Act 2000 (establishments and agencies);

   (b) under Part IV of that Act (social care workers); or

   (c) for child minding or providing day care under Part XA of the Children Act 1989, or under section 71 of that Act or Article 118 of the Children (Northern Ireland) Order 1995 (child minding and day care)."   1989 c. 41. S.I. 1995/755 (N.I. 2).

(3) In section 115 (enhanced criminal record certificates)—

   (a) in subsection (5)—

      (i) after paragraph (e) there shall be inserted—

"(ea) registration under Part II of the Care Standards Act 2000 (establishments and agencies);

(eb) registration under Part IV of that Act (social care workers);"; and

      (ii) after paragraph (g) there shall be inserted—

"(h) a decision made by an adoption agency within the meaning of section 11 of the Adoption Act 1976 as to a person's suitability to adopt a child."; and   1976 c. 36.

(b) in subsection (6A), after "113," there shall be inserted "or his suitability to adopt a child,".

PART VIII

MISCELLANEOUS

Boarding schools and colleges

Welfare of
children in
boarding schools
and colleges.

105.—(1) Section 87 of the 1989 Act (welfare of children accommodated in independent schools) shall be amended in accordance with subsections (2) to (4).

(2) For subsections (1) to (5) there shall be substituted—

"(1) Where a school or college provides accommodation for any child, it shall be the duty of the relevant person to safeguard and promote the child's welfare.

(2) Subsection (1) does not apply in relation to a school or college which is a children's home or care home.

(3) Where accommodation is provided for a child by any school or college the appropriate authority shall take such steps as are reasonably practicable to enable them to determine whether the child's welfare is adequately safeguarded and promoted while he is accommodated by the school or college.

(4) Where the Commission are of the opinion that there has been a failure to comply with subsection (1) in relation to a child provided with accommodation by a school or college, they shall—

(a) in the case of a school other than an independent school or a special school, notify the local education authority for the area in which the school is situated;

(b) in the case of a special school which is maintained by a local education authority, notify that authority;

(c) in any other case, notify the Secretary of State.

(4A) Where the National Assembly for Wales are of the opinion that there has been a failure to comply with subsection (1) in relation to a child provided with accommodation by a school or college, they shall—

(a) in the case of a school other than an independent school or a special school, notify the local education authority for the area in which the school is situated;

(b) in the case of a special school which is maintained by a local education authority, notify that authority.

(5) Where accommodation is, or is to be, provided for a child by any school or college, a person authorised by the appropriate authority may, for the purpose of enabling that authority to discharge its duty under this section, enter at any time premises which are, or are to be, premises of the school or college."

(3) In subsection (6), for "entering an independent school in exercise of" there shall be substituted "exercising".

(4) For subsection (10) there shall be substituted—

"(10) In this section and sections 87A to 87D—

"the 1992 Act" means the Further and Higher Education Act 1992;

"appropriate authority" means—

> (a) in relation to England, the National Care Standards Commission;

> (b) in relation to Wales, the National Assembly for Wales;

"college" means an institution within the further education sector as defined in section 91 of the 1992 Act;

"the Commission" means the National Care Standards Commission;

"further education corporation" has the same meaning as in the 1992 Act;

"local education authority" and "proprietor" have the same meanings as in the Education Act 1996".

(11) In this section and sections 87A and 87D "relevant person" means—

> (a) in relation to an independent school, the proprietor of the school;

> (b) in relation to any other school, or an institution designated under section 28 of the 1992 Act, the governing body of the school or institution;

> (c) in relation to an institution conducted by a further education corporation, the corporation.

(12) Where a person other than the proprietor of an independent school is responsible for conducting the school, references in this section to the relevant person include references to the person so responsible."

(5) In section 62 of the 1989 Act (duties of local authorities in relation to children provided with accommodation by voluntary organisations), at the end there shall be inserted—

"(10) This section does not apply in relation to any voluntary organisation which is an institution within the further education sector, as defined in section 91 of the Further and Higher Education Act 1992, or a school."

106.—(1) For section 87A of the 1989 Act (suspension of duty under section 87(3)) there shall be substituted—   Suspension of duty under section 87(3) of the 1989 Act.

"Suspension of duty under section 87(3).   87A.—(1) The Secretary of State may appoint a person to be an inspector for the purposes of this section if—

> (a) that person already acts as an inspector for other purposes in relation to schools or colleges to which section 87(1) applies, and

> (b) the Secretary of State is satisfied that the person is an appropriate person to determine whether the welfare of children provided with accommodation by such schools or colleges is adequately safeguarded and promoted while they are accommodated by them.

(2) Where—

(a) the relevant person enters into an agreement in writing with a person appointed under subsection (1),

(b) the agreement provides for the person so appointed to have in relation to the school or college the function of determining whether section 87(1) is being complied with, and

(c) the appropriate authority receive from the person mentioned in paragraph (b) ("the inspector") notice in writing that the agreement has come into effect,

the appropriate authority's duty under section 87(3) in relation to the school or college shall be suspended.

(3) Where the appropriate authority's duty under section 87(3) in relation to any school or college is suspended under this section, it shall cease to be so suspended if the appropriate authority receive—

(a) a notice under subsection (4) relating to the inspector, or

(b) a notice under subsection (5) relating to the relevant agreement.

(4) The Secretary of State shall terminate a person's appointment under subsection (1) if—

(a) that person so requests, or

(b) the Secretary of State ceases, in relation to that person, to be satisfied that he is such a person as is mentioned in paragraph (b) of that subsection,

and shall give notice of the termination of that person's appointment to the appropriate authority.

(5) Where—

(a) the appropriate authority's duty under section 87(3) in relation to any school or college is suspended under this section, and

(b) the relevant agreement ceases to have effect,

the inspector shall give to the appropriate authority notice in writing of the fact that it has ceased to have effect.

(6) In this section references to the relevant agreement, in relation to the suspension of the appropriate authority's duty under section 87(3) as regards any school or college, are to the agreement by virtue of which the appropriate authority's duty under that provision as regards that school or college is suspended."

(2) In section 87B of that Act (duties of inspectors under section 87A)—

(a) in subsections (2) and (3), after "school", in each place where it occurs, there shall be inserted "or college";

    (b) in subsection (2), for "to the Secretary of State" there shall be substituted—

        "(a) in the case of a school other than an independent school or a special school, to the local education authority for the area in which the school is situated;

        (b) in the case of a special school which is maintained by a local education authority, to that authority;

        (c) in any other case, to the Secretary of State"; and

    (c) for subsection (4) there shall be substituted the following subsection—

    "(4) In this section "substitution agreement" means an agreement by virtue of which the duty of the appropriate authority under section 87(3) in relation to a school or college is suspended."

107. After section 87B of the 1989 Act there shall be inserted—

Boarding schools: national minimum standards.

    87C.—(1) The Secretary of State may prepare and publish statements of national minimum standards for safeguarding and promoting the welfare of children for whom accommodation is provided in a school or college.

    (2) The Secretary of State shall keep the standards set out in the statements under review and may publish amended statements whenever he considers it appropriate to do so.

    (3) Before issuing a statement, or an amended statement which in the opinion of the Secretary of State effects a substantial change in the standards, the Secretary of State shall consult any persons he considers appropriate.

    (4) The standards shall be taken into account—

        (a) in the making by the appropriate authority of any determination under section 87(4) or (4A);

        (b) in the making by a person appointed under section 87A(1) of any determination under section 87B(2); and

        (c) in any proceedings under any other enactment in which it is alleged that the person has failed to comply with section 87(1)."

Boarding schools: national minimum standards.

108. After section 87C of the 1989 Act (inserted by section 107) there shall be inserted—

Annual fee for boarding school inspections.

    87D.—(1) Regulations under subsection (2) may be made in relation to any school or college in respect of which the appropriate authority is required to take steps under section 87(3).

    (2) The Secretary of State may by regulations require the relevant person to pay the appropriate authority an annual fee of such amount, and within such time, as the regulations may specify.

Annual fee for boarding school inspections.

(3) A fee payable by virtue of this section may, without prejudice to any other method of recovery, be recovered summarily as a civil debt."

Inspection of schools etc. by persons authorised by Secretary of State.

109.—(1) Section 80 of the 1989 Act (inspection of children's homes etc. by persons authorised by Secretary of State) shall be amended as follows.

(2) In subsection (1), in paragraph (l), for "independent school" there shall be substituted "school or college".

(3) In subsection (5)—

(a) in paragraph (d), at the end there shall be inserted "or governing body of any other school";

(b) after that paragraph there shall be inserted—

1992 c. 13.

"(da) governing body of an institution designated under section 28 of the Further and Higher Education Act 1992;

(db) further education corporation;" and

(c) after paragraph (i) there shall be inserted—

"(j) person carrying on a fostering agency."

(4) After subsection (12) there shall be inserted—

"(13) In this section—

"college" means an institution within the further education sector as defined in section 91 of the Further and Higher Education Act 1992;

"fostering agency" has the same meaning as in the Care Standards Act 2000;

"further education corporation" has the same meaning as in the Further and Higher Education Act 1992."

Fostering

Extension of Part IX to school children during holidays.

110. In paragraph 9(1) of Schedule 8 to the 1989 Act (extension of Part IX to certain school children during holidays), "which is not maintained by a local education authority" shall be omitted.

Employment agencies

Nurses Agencies.
1957 c. 16.
1973 c. 35.

111.—(1) The Nurses Agencies Act 1957 shall cease to have effect.

(2) In section 13 of the Employment Agencies Act 1973 (interpretation), for subsection (8) there shall be substituted—

"(8) This Act, in its application to Scotland, does not apply to—

1951 c. 55.

(a) any agency for the supply of nurses as defined in section 32 of the Nurses (Scotland) Act 1951 (but excluding any other business carried on in conjunction with such an agency);

(b) the business carried on by any county or district nursing association or other similar organisation, being an association or organisation within paragraph (a) or (b) of that definition.",

and paragraphs (b) and (c) of, and the proviso to, subsection (7) shall be omitted.

Charges for local authority welfare services

112. In Schedule 1 to the Local Authority Social Services Act 1970 (enactments conferring functions assigned to social services committee), there shall be inserted at the appropriate place—

"Health and Social Services and Social Security Adjudications Act 1983 (c. 41)	Charges for local authority welfare services".
Section 17, so far as relating to services provided under the enactments mentioned in subsection (2)(a) to (c)	

Charges for local authority welfare services.
1970 c. 42.

PART IX

GENERAL AND SUPPLEMENTAL

CHAPTER I

GENERAL

113.—(1) The powers conferred by this section are exercisable by the Secretary of State if he is satisfied that the Commission or the English Council—

    (a) has without reasonable excuse failed to discharge any of its functions; or

    (b) in discharging any of its functions, has without reasonable excuse failed to comply with any directions or guidance given by him under section 6(2) or 54(4) in relation to those functions.

(2) The powers conferred by this section are exercisable by the Assembly if it is satisfied that the Welsh Council—

    (a) has without reasonable excuse failed to discharge any of its functions; or

    (b) in discharging any of its functions, has without reasonable excuse failed to comply with any directions or guidance given by the Assembly under section 54(4) in relation to those functions.

(3) The appropriate Minister may—

    (a) make an order declaring the authority in question to be in default; and

    (b) direct the authority to discharge such of its functions, and in such manner and within such period or periods, as may be specified in the direction.

(4) If the authority fails to comply with the appropriate Minister's direction under subsection (3), the appropriate Minister may—

    (a) discharge the functions to which the direction relates himself; or

    (b) make arrangements for any other person to discharge those functions on his behalf.

Default powers of appropriate Minister.

114.—(1) This section and the next apply to a scheme made under section 38, 70 or 79(3) for transferring eligible employees.

(2) Subject to those provisions, such a scheme may apply to all, or any description of, employees or to any individual employee.

Schemes for the transfer of staff.

(3) Such a scheme may be made by the appropriate Minister, and a recommendation may be made to Her Majesty in Council to make an Order containing such a scheme, only if any prescribed requirements about consultation have been complied with in relation to each of the employees to be transferred under the scheme.

Effect of schemes.   **115.**—(1) The contract of employment of an employee transferred under the scheme—

(a) is not terminated by the transfer; and

(b) has effect from the date of transfer as if originally made between the employee and the transferee.

(2) Where an employee is transferred under the scheme—

(a) all the rights, powers, duties and liabilities of the old employer under or in connection with the contract of employment are by virtue of this subsection transferred to the transferee on the date of transfer; and

(b) anything done before that date by or in relation to the old employer in respect of that contract or the employee is to be treated from that date as having been done by or in relation to the transferee.

This subsection does not prejudice the generality of subsection (1).

(3) Subsections (1) and (2) do not transfer an employee's contract of employment, or the rights, powers, duties and liabilities under or in connection with it, if he informs the old employer or the transferee that he objects to the transfer.

(4) Where an employee objects as mentioned in subsection (3), his contract of employment with the old employer is terminated immediately before the date of transfer; but he is not to be treated, for any purpose, as having been dismissed by that employer.

(5) This section does not prejudice any right of an employee to terminate his contract of employment if a substantial change is made to his detriment in his working conditions.

But no such right arises by reason only that, by virtue of this section, the identity of his employer changes unless the employee shows that, in all the circumstances, the change is a significant change and is to his detriment.

(6) In this section—

"date of transfer" means the date of transfer determined under the scheme in relation to the employee;

"transferee" means the new employer to whom the employee is or would be transferred under the scheme;

and expressions used in this section and in the provision under which the scheme is made have the same meaning as in that provision.

Minor and consequential amendments.   **116.** Schedule 4 (which makes minor amendments and amendments consequential on the provisions of this Act) shall have effect.

117.—(1) Schedule 5 (which makes transitional and saving provision) shall have effect; but nothing in that Schedule shall be taken to prejudice the operation of sections 16 and 17 of the Interpretation Act 1978 (which relate to the effect of repeals).

(2) The enactments mentioned in Schedule 6 to this Act are repealed to the extent specified in that Schedule.

CHAPTER II

SUPPLEMENTAL

118.—(1) Any power conferred on the Secretary of State, the Assembly or the appropriate Minister to make regulations or an order under this Act except an order under section 38 or 79(3) shall be exercised by statutory instrument.

(2) An order making any provision by virtue of section 119(2) which adds to, replaces or omits any part of the text of an Act shall not be made by the Secretary of State unless a draft of the instrument has been laid before, and approved by resolution of, each House of Parliament.

(3) Subject to subsection (2), an instrument containing regulations or an order made by the Secretary of State, except an instrument containing an order under section 122, shall be subject to annulment in pursuance of a resolution of either House of Parliament.

In subsection (2) and this subsection, references to the Secretary of State include the Secretary of State and the Assembly acting jointly.

(4) Subsections (5) to (7) apply to any power of the Secretary of State, the Assembly or the appropriate Minister to make regulations or an order under this Act; and subsections (5) and (6) apply to any power of Her Majesty to make an Order in Council under section 70.

(5) The power may be exercised either in relation to all cases to which the power extends, or in relation to all those cases subject to specified exceptions, or in relation to any specified cases or classes of case.

(6) The power may be exercised so as to make, as respects the cases in relation to which it is exercised—

    (a) the same provision for all cases in relation to which the power is exercised, or different provision for different cases or different classes of case, or different provision as respects the same case or class of case for different purposes;

    (b) any such provision either unconditionally or subject to any specified condition.

(7) The power may be exercised so as to make—

    (a) any supplementary, incidental or consequential provision,

    (b) any transitory, transitional or saving provision,

which the person exercising the power considers necessary or expedient.

(8) The provision which, by virtue of subsection (7), may be made by regulations under the Part of this Act which relates to the Children's Commissioner for Wales includes provision amending or repealing any enactment or instrument.

Supplementary
and consequential
provision etc.

119.—(1) The appropriate Minister may by order make—

(a) any supplementary, incidental or consequential provision,

(b) any transitory, transitional or saving provision,

which he considers necessary or expedient for the purposes of, in consequence of or for giving full effect to any provision of this Act.

(2) The provision which may be made under subsection (1) includes provision amending or repealing any enactment or instrument.

Wales.
1998 c. 38.

120.—(1) Section 84(1) of the Government of Wales Act 1998 (payment of Assembly receipts into the Consolidated Fund) does not apply to any sums received by the Assembly by virtue of any provision of this Act.

S.I. 1999/672.

(2) The reference to the 1989 Act in Schedule 1 to the National Assembly for Wales (Transfer of Functions) Order 1999 is to be treated as referring to that Act as amended by or under this Act.

(3) Subsection (2) does not affect the power to make further Orders varying or omitting that reference.

General
interpretation etc.

121.—(1) In this Act—

"adult" means a person who is not a child;

"appropriate Minister" means—

(a) in relation to England, Scotland or Northern Ireland, the Secretary of State;

(b) in relation to Wales, the Assembly;

and in relation to England and Wales means the Secretary of State and the Assembly acting jointly;

"child" means a person under the age of 18;

"community home" has the same meaning as in the 1989 Act;

1973 c. 35.

"employment agency" and "employment business" have the same meanings as in the Employment Agencies Act 1973; but no business which is an employment business shall be taken to be an employment agency;

1978 c. 30.

"enactment" includes an enactment comprised in subordinate legislation (within the meaning of the Interpretation Act 1978);

"to foster a child privately" has the same meaning as in the 1989 Act;

"harm"—

(a) in relation to an adult who is not mentally impaired, means ill-treatment or the impairment of health;

(b) in relation to an adult who is mentally impaired, or a child, means ill-treatment or the impairment of health or development;

1977 c. 49.

"health service hospital" has the same meaning as in the National Health Service Act 1977;

"illness" includes any injury;

1996 c. 56.

"independent school" has the same meaning as in the Education Act 1996;

"local authority" has the same meaning as in the 1989 Act;

"local authority foster parent" has the same meaning as in the 1989 Act;

"medical" includes surgical;

"mental disorder" means mental illness, arrested or incomplete development of mind, psychopathic disorder, and any other disorder or disability of mind;

"National Health Service body" means a National Health Service trust, a Health Authority, a Special Health Authority or a Primary Care Trust;

"parent", in relation to a child, includes any person who is not a parent of his but who has parental responsibility for him;

"parental responsibility" has the same meaning as in the 1989 Act;

"prescribed" means prescribed by regulations;

"proprietor", in relation to a school, has the same meaning as in the Education Act 1996;

1996 c. 56.

"regulations" (except where provision is made for them to be made by the Secretary of State or the Assembly) means regulations made by the appropriate Minister;

"relative" has the same meaning as in the 1989 Act;

"school" has the same meaning as in the Education Act 1996;

"social services functions" means functions which are social services functions for the purposes of the Local Authority Social Services Act 1970;

1970 c. 42.

"treatment" includes diagnosis;

"the Tribunal" means the tribunal established by section 9 of the 1999 Act;

"undertaking" includes any business or profession and—

    (a) in relation to a public or local authority, includes the exercise of any functions of that authority; and

    (b) in relation to any other body of persons, whether corporate or unincorporate, includes any of the activities of that body;

"voluntary organisation" has the same meaning as in the Adoption Act 1976.

(2) For the purposes of this Act—

(a) a person is disabled if—

    (i) his sight, hearing or speech is substantially impaired;

    (ii) he has a mental disorder; or

    (iii) he is physically substantially disabled by any illness, any impairment present since birth, or otherwise;

(b) an adult is mentally impaired if he is in a state of arrested or incomplete development of mind (including a significant impairment of intelligence and social functioning).

(3) In this Act, the expression "personal care" does not include any prescribed activity.

(4) For the purposes of this Act, the person who carries on a fostering agency falling within section 4(4)(b), or a voluntary adoption agency, is the voluntary organisation itself.

(5) References in this Act to a person who carries on an establishment or agency include references to a person who carries it on otherwise than for profit.

(6) For the purposes of this Act, a community home which is provided by a voluntary organisation shall be taken to be carried on by—

(a) the person who equips and maintains it; and

(b) if the appropriate Minister determines that the body of managers for the home, or a specified member of that body, is also to be treated as carrying on the home, that body or member.

(7) Where a community home is provided by a voluntary organisation, the appropriate Minister may determine that for the purposes of this Act the home is to be taken to be managed solely by—

(a) any specified member of the body of managers for the home; or

(b) any other specified person on whom functions are conferred under the home's instrument of management.

(8) A determination under subsection (6) or (7) may be made either generally or in relation to a particular home or class of homes.

(9) An establishment is not a care home for the purposes of this Act unless the care which it provides includes assistance with bodily functions where such assistance is required.

(10) References in this Act to a child's being looked after by a local authority shall be construed in accordance with section 22 of the 1989 Act.

(11) For the purposes of this Act an individual is made redundant if—

(a) he is dismissed; and

1996 c. 18.

(b) for the purposes of the Employment Rights Act 1996 the dismissal is by reason of redundancy.

(12) Any register kept for the purposes of this Act may be kept by means of a computer.

(13) In this Act, the expressions listed in the left-hand column have the meaning given by, or are to be interpreted in accordance with, the provisions listed in the right-hand column.

	Expression	*Provision of this Act*
1989 c. 41.	1989 Act	Children Act 1989
1999 c. 14.	1999 Act	Protection of Children Act 1999
	Assembly	Section 5
	Care home	Section 3
	CCETSW	Section 70
	Children's home	Section 1
	Commission	Section 6
	Commissioner	Section 72
	Council, the English Council, the Welsh Council	Section 54
	Domiciliary care agency	Section 4
	Fostering agency	Section 4

Hospital and independent hospital	Section 2
Independent clinic and independent medical agency	Section 2
Registration authority	Section 5
Residential family centre	Section 4
Voluntary adoption agency	Section 4

122. This Act, except section 70(2) to (5) and this Chapter, shall come into force on such day as the appropriate Minister may by order appoint, and different days may be appointed for different purposes.

Commencement.

123.—(1) This Act may be cited as the Care Standards Act 2000.

(2) Subject to subsections (3) and (4), this Act extends to England and Wales only.

(3) Section 70 and, so far as relating to subsections (2) to (5) of that section, sections 114, 115 and 118 extend also to Scotland and Northern Ireland.

(4) The amendment or repeal by this Act of an enactment extending to Scotland or Northern Ireland extends also to Scotland or, as the case may be, Northern Ireland.

Short title and extent.

SCHEDULES

SCHEDULE 1

THE COMMISSION AND THE COUNCILS

Introductory

1.—(1) The authorities for the purposes of this Schedule are the Commission, the English Council and the Welsh Council.

(2) In this Schedule, in relation to the Welsh Council—

(a) references to the Secretary of State or to Parliament are to be read as references to the Assembly;

(b) references to the Comptroller and Auditor General are to be read as references to the Auditor General for Wales.

Status

2. An authority is not to be regarded as the servant or agent of the Crown or as enjoying any status, immunity or privilege of the Crown; and an authority's property is to not to be regarded as property of, or property held on behalf of, the Crown.

General powers

3.—(1) Subject to any directions given by the Secretary of State, an authority may do anything which appears to it to be necessary or expedient for the purpose of, or in connection with, the exercise of its functions.

(2) That includes, in particular—

(a) co-operating with other public authorities in the United Kingdom;

(b) acquiring and disposing of land and other property; and

(c) entering into contracts.

General duty

4. It is the duty of an authority to carry out its functions effectively, efficiently and economically.

Membership

5. Each authority is to consist of a chairman and other members appointed by the Secretary of State.

Appointment, procedure etc.

6. The Secretary of State may by regulations make provision as to—

(a) the appointment of the chairman and other members of an authority (including the number, or limits on the number, of members who may be appointed and any conditions to be fulfilled for appointment);

(b) the tenure of office of the chairman and other members of an authority (including the circumstances in which they cease to hold office or may be removed or suspended from office);

(c) the appointment of, constitution of and exercise of functions by committees and sub-committees of an authority (including committees and sub-committees which consist of or include persons who are not members of the authority); and

(d) the procedure of an authority and any committees or sub-committees of an authority (including the validation of proceedings in the event of vacancies or defects in appointment).

Remuneration and allowances

7.—(1) An authority may pay to its chairman, to any other member of the authority and to any member of a committee or sub-committee who is not a member of the authority, such remuneration and allowances as the Secretary of State may determine.

(2) If the Secretary of State so determines, an authority must pay or make provision for the payment of such pension, allowance or gratuities as the Secretary of State may determine to or in respect of a person who is or has been the chairman or any other member of an authority.

(3) If the Secretary of State determines that there are special circumstances that make it right for a person ceasing to hold office as chairman of an authority to receive compensation, the authority must pay to him or make provision for the payment to him of such compensation as the Secretary of State may determine.

Chief officer

8.—(1) There is to be a chief officer of each authority who is to be a member of the staff of the authority and is to be responsible to the authority for the general exercise of its functions.

(2) The first chief officer is to be appointed by the Secretary of State on such terms and conditions as the Secretary of State may determine.

(3) Any subsequent chief officer is to be appointed by the authority.

(4) An appointment under sub-paragraph (3) requires the approval of the Secretary of State.

Regional directors

9.—(1) The Secretary of State may direct the Commission to appoint directors for regions specified in the direction.

(2) Directors appointed under sub-paragraph (1) shall be members of the staff of the Commission and shall have such functions as may be prescribed.

Children's rights director

10.—(1) The Commission shall appoint a children's rights director who is to be a member of the staff of the Commission.

(2) The children's rights director shall have such functions as may be prescribed.

Director of private and voluntary health care

11.—(1) The Commission shall appoint a director of private and voluntary health care, who is to be a member of the staff of the Commission.

(2) The director shall have such functions as may be prescribed.

Staff

12.—(1) An authority may appoint such other staff as it considers appropriate.

(2) Subject to sub-paragraph (4), staff appointed by an authority are to be appointed on such terms and conditions as the authority may determine.

(3) Without prejudice to its powers apart from this paragraph, an authority may pay, or make provision for the payment of—

(a) pensions, allowances or gratuities;

(b) compensation for loss of employment or for reduction of remuneration,

to or in respect of staff appointed by them.

(4) The Secretary of State may give directions as to—

  (a) the appointment of staff by an authority (including any conditions to be fulfilled for appointment);

  (b) their terms and conditions; and

  (c) any other provision that may be made by the authority under sub-paragraph (3).

(5) Sub-paragraphs (3) and (4)(c) apply to the first chief officer as they apply to other staff.

(6) Different directions may be given under sub-paragraph (4) in relation to different categories of staff.

Delegation of functions

13.—(1) An authority may arrange for the discharge of any of its functions by a committee, sub-committee, member or member of staff of the authority.

(2) An authority may make arrangements with persons under which they, or members of their staff, may perform functions of members of the staff of the authority.

Arrangements for the use of staff

14. The Secretary of State may by regulations provide for arrangements under which—

  (a) members of staff of an authority are placed at the disposal of a prescribed person for the purpose of discharging, or assisting in the discharge of, prescribed functions of that person; or

  (b) members of staff of a prescribed person are placed at the disposal of an authority for the purpose of discharging, or assisting in the discharge of, any functions of the authority.

Training

15. The Commission may provide training for the purpose of assisting persons to attain standards set out in any statements published by the Secretary of State under section 23.

Payments to authorities

16. The Secretary of State may make payments to an authority of such amounts, at such times and on such conditions (if any) as he considers appropriate.

Fees

17.—(1) Subject to the provisions of this Act, the Commission may not, except with the consent of the Secretary of State, charge a fee in connection with the exercise of any power conferred on it by or under this Act.

(2) The Commission may charge a reasonable fee determined by it—

  (a) for any advice, forms or documents provided for the assistance of a person who proposes to apply, or is considering whether to apply, for registration under Part II; and

  (b) for any training provided by it under paragraph 15.

(3) The consent of the Secretary of State for the purposes of sub-paragraph (1) may be given in relation to the exercise of a power either generally or in a particular case.

Accounts

18.—(1) An authority must keep accounts in such form as the Secretary of State may determine.

(2) An authority must prepare annual accounts in respect of each financial year in such form as the Secretary of State may determine.

(3) An authority must send copies of the annual accounts to the Secretary of State and the Comptroller and Auditor General within such period after the end of the financial year to which the accounts relate as the Secretary of State may determine.

(4) The Comptroller and Auditor General must examine, certify and report on the annual accounts and must lay copies of the accounts and of his report before Parliament.

(5) In this paragraph and paragraph 19 "financial year", in relation to an authority, means—

(a) the period beginning with the date on which the authority is established and ending with the next 31st March following that date; and

(b) each successive period of twelve months ending with 31st March.

Reports and other information

19.—(1) As soon as possible after the end of each financial year, an authority must make a report to the Secretary of State on the exercise of its functions during the year.

(2) An authority must provide the Secretary of State with such reports and information relating to the exercise of its functions as he may from time to time require.

(3) A report made under sub-paragraph (1) must be published in a manner which the authority considers appropriate.

Application of seal and evidence

20. The application of the seal of an authority must be authenticated by the signature—

(a) of any member of the authority; or

(b) of any other person who has been authorised by the authority (whether generally or specifically) for that purpose.

21. A document purporting to be duly executed under the seal of an authority or to be signed on its behalf is to be received in evidence and, unless the contrary is proved, taken to be so executed or signed.

General

22. In Schedule 1 to the Public Records Act 1958 (definition of public records), the following entries shall be inserted at the appropriate places in Part II of the Table at the end of paragraph 3—

1958 c. 51.

"Care Council for Wales."

"General Social Care Council."

"National Care Standards Commission."

1960 c. 67.

23. In the Schedule to the Public Bodies (Admission to Meetings) Act 1960 (bodies to which the Act applies), after paragraph (bc) of paragraph 1 there shall be inserted—

"(bd) the Care Council for Wales;

(be) the General Social Care Council;

(bf) the National Care Standards Commission;".

1967 c. 13.

24. In the Parliamentary Commissioner Act 1967, in Schedule 2 (departments and authorities subject to investigation), the following entries shall be inserted at the appropriate places—

"General Social Care Council."

"National Care Standards Commission."

1975 c. 24.

25. In the House of Commons Disqualification Act 1975, in Part II of Schedule 1 (bodies of which all members are disqualified), the following entries shall be inserted at the appropriate places—

"The Care Council for Wales."

"The General Social Care Council."

"The National Care Standards Commission."

1975 c. 25.

26. In the Northern Ireland Assembly Disqualification Act 1975, the same entries as are set out in paragraph 25 are inserted at the appropriate places in Part II of Schedule 1.

1998 c. 38.

27. In the Government of Wales Act 1998—

(a) in section 118(2) (meaning of "Welsh public records"), after "referred to in subsection (1)(e) are—" there shall be inserted—

"(aa) the Care Council for Wales;"

(b) in Schedule 4 (public bodies subject to reform by Assembly), after paragraph 3 there shall be inserted—

"3A. The Care Council for Wales."

(c) in paragraph 14(2) of Schedule 9 (bodies subject to investigation by the Welsh Administration Ombudsman), after paragraph (a) there shall be inserted—

"(ab) the Care Council for Wales;" and

(d) in paragraph 1 of Schedule 17 (audit of Welsh public bodies), at the end there shall be inserted "(other than the Care Council for Wales)".

Section 72.

SCHEDULE 2

THE CHILDREN'S COMMISSIONER FOR WALES

Status

1.—(1) The Commissioner is to be a corporation sole.

(2) The Commissioner is not to be regarded as the servant or agent or the Crown or as enjoying any status, immunity or privilege of the Crown; and the Commissioner's property is not to be regarded as property of, or property held on behalf of, the Crown.

Appointment and tenure of office

2. Regulations may make provision—

　(a) as to the appointment of the Commissioner (including any conditions to be fulfilled for appointment);

　(b) as to the filling of vacancies in the office of Commissioner;

　(c) as to the tenure of office of the Commissioner (including the circumstances in which he ceases to hold office or may be removed or suspended from office).

Remuneration

3. The Assembly shall—

　(a) pay the Commissioner such remuneration and allowances; and

　(b) pay, or make provision for the payment of, such pension or gratuities to or in respect of him,

as may be provided for under the terms of his appointment.

Staff

4.—(1) The Commissioner may appoint any staff he considers necessary for assisting him in the exercise of his functions, one of whom shall be appointed as deputy Commissioner.

(2) During any vacancy in the office of Commissioner or at any time when the Commissioner is for any reason unable to act, the deputy Commissioner shall exercise his functions (and any property or rights vested in the Commissioner may accordingly be dealt with by the deputy as if vested in him).

(3) Without prejudice to sub-paragraph (2), any member of the Commissioner's staff may, so far as authorised by him, exercise any of his functions.

General powers

5.—(1) Subject to any directions given by the Assembly, the Commissioner may do anything which appears to him to be necessary or expedient for the purpose of, or in connection with, the exercise of his functions.

(2) That includes, in particular—

　(a) co-operating with other public authorities in the United Kingdom;

　(b) acquiring and disposing of land and other property; and

　(c) entering into contracts.

Estimates

6.—(1) For each financial year after the first, the Commissioner shall prepare, and submit to the executive committee, an estimate of his income and expenses.

(2) Each such estimate shall be submitted to the executive committee at least five months before the beginning of the financial year to which it relates.

(3) The executive committee shall examine each such estimate submitted to it and, after having done so, shall lay the estimate before the Assembly with any such modifications as the committee thinks fit.

(4) Regulations shall specify the periods which are to be treated as the first and subsequent financial years of the Commissioner.

(5) In this paragraph and paragraph 10 "executive committee" has the same meaning as in the Government of Wales Act 1998.　　　　1998 c. 38.

Accounts

7.—(1) The Commissioner shall keep proper accounting records.

(2) The Commissioner shall prepare accounts for each financial year in such form as the Assembly may with the consent of the Treasury determine.

Reports

8. Regulations may provide for the Commissioner to make periodic or other reports to the Assembly relating to the exercise of his functions and may require the reports to be published in the manner required by the regulations.

Audit

9.—(1) The accounts prepared by the Commissioner for any financial year shall be submitted by him to the Auditor General for Wales not more than five months after the end of that year.

(2) The Auditor General for Wales shall—

  (a) examine and certify any accounts submitted to him under this paragraph; and

  (b) no later than four months after the accounts are submitted to him, lay before the Assembly a copy of them as certified by him together with his report on them.

(3) In examining any accounts submitted to him under this paragraph, the Auditor General for Wales shall, in particular, satisfy himself that the expenditure to which the accounts relate has been incurred lawfully and in accordance with the authority which governs it.

Accounting officer

10.—(1) The accounting officer for the Commissioner's Office shall be the Commissioner.

(2) The accounting officer for the Commissioner shall have, in relation to the accounts of the Commissioner and the finances of the Commissioner's Office, the responsibilities which are from time to time specified by the Treasury.

(3) In this paragraph references to responsibilities include in particular—

  (a) responsibilities in relation to the signing of accounts;

  (b) responsibilities for the propriety and regularity of the finances of the Commissioner's Office; and

  (c) responsibilities for the economy, efficiency and effectiveness with which the resources of the Commissioner's Office are used.

(4) The responsibilities which may be specified under this paragraph include responsibilities owed to—

  (a) the Assembly, the executive committee or the Audit Committee; or

  (b) the House of Commons or its Committee of Public Accounts.

(5) If requested to do so by the House of Commons Committee of Public Accounts, the Audit Committee may—

  (a) on behalf of the Committee of Public Accounts take evidence from the accounting officer for the Commissioner's Office; and

  (b) report to the Committee of Public Accounts and transmit to that Committee any evidence so taken.

(6) In this paragraph and paragraphs 11 and 12 "the Commissioner's Office" means the Commissioner and the members of his staff.

Examinations into use of resources

11.—(1) The Auditor General for Wales may carry out examinations into the economy, efficiency and effectiveness with which the Commissioner has used the resources of the Commissioner's Office in discharging his functions.

(2) Sub-paragraph (1) shall not be construed as entitling the Auditor General for Wales to question the merits of the policy objectives of the Commissioner.

(3) In determining how to exercise his functions under this paragraph, the Auditor General for Wales shall take into account the views of the Audit Committee as to the examinations which he should carry out under this paragraph.

(4) The Auditor General for Wales may lay before the Assembly a report of the results of any examination carried out by him under this paragraph.

(5) The Auditor General for Wales and the Comptroller and Auditor General may co-operate with, and give assistance to, each other in connection with the carrying out of examinations in respect of the Commissioner under this paragraph or section 7 of the National Audit Act 1983 (economy etc. examinations).

1983 c. 44.

Examinations by the Comptroller and Auditor General

12.—(1) For the purpose of enabling him to carry out examinations into, and report to Parliament on, the finances of the Commissioner's Office, the Comptroller and Auditor General—

(a) shall have a right of access at all reasonable times to all such documents in the custody or under the control of the Commissioner, or of the Auditor General for Wales, as he may reasonably require for that purpose; and

(b) shall be entitled to require from any person holding or accountable for any of those documents any assistance, information or explanation which he reasonably thinks necessary for that purpose.

(2) The Comptroller and Auditor General shall—

(a) consult the Auditor General for Wales; and

(b) take into account any relevant work done or being done by the Auditor General for Wales,

before he acts in reliance on sub-paragraph (1) or carries out an examination in respect of the Commissioner under section 7 of the National Audit Act 1983 (economy etc. examinations).

Evidence

13. A document purporting to be duly executed under the seal of the Commissioner or to be signed by him or on his behalf is to be received in evidence and, unless the contrary is proved, taken to be so executed or signed.

Payments

14. The Assembly may make payments to the Commissioner of such amounts, at such times and on such conditions (if any) as it considers appropriate.

General

15. In the House of Commons Disqualification Act 1975, in Part III of Schedule 1 (certain disqualifying offices), the following entries are inserted at the appropriate places—

1975 c. 24.

"Children's Commissioner for Wales."

"Member of the staff of the Children's Commissioner for Wales."

1975 c. 25.

16. In the Northern Ireland Assembly Disqualification Act 1975, the same entries as are set out in paragraph 15 are inserted at the appropriate places in Part III of Schedule 1.

17.—(1) Regulations may provide that the office of Children's Commissioner for Wales shall be added to the list of "Offices" in Schedule 1 to the Superannuation Act 1972 (offices etc. to which section 1 of that Act applies).

1972 c. 11.

(2) The Assembly shall pay to the Minister for the Civil Service, at such times as he may direct, such sums as he may determine in respect of any increase attributable to provision made under sub-paragraph (1) in the sums payable out of money provided by Parliament under the Superannuation Act 1972.

1998 c. 38.

18. In section 144 of the Government of Wales Act 1998 (accounts etc.), in subsection (8)(a), after "the Welsh Administration Ombudsman" there shall be inserted "the Children's Commissioner for Wales".

Section 79.

SCHEDULE 3

CHILD MINDING AND DAY CARE FOR YOUNG CHILDREN

The following Schedule shall be inserted in the 1989 Act after Schedule 9—

"SCHEDULE 9A

CHILD MINDING AND DAY CARE FOR YOUNG CHILDREN

Exemption of certain schools

1.—(1) Except in prescribed circumstances, Part XA does not apply to provision of day care within sub-paragraph (2) for any child looked after in—

    (a) a maintained school;

    (b) a school assisted by a local education authority;

    (c) a school in respect of which payments are made by the Secretary of State or the Assembly under section 485 of the Education Act 1996;

1996 c. 56.

    (d) an independent school.

(2) The provision mentioned in sub-paragraph (1) is provision of day care made by—

    (a) the person carrying on the establishment in question as part of the establishment's activities; or

    (b) a person employed to work at that establishment and authorised to make that provision as part of the establishment's activities.

(3) In sub-paragraph (1)—

"assisted" has the same meaning as in the Education Act 1996;

"maintained school" has the meaning given by section 20(7) of the School Standards and Framework Act 1998.

1998 c. 31.

Exemption for other establishments

2.—(1) Part XA does not apply to provision of day care within sub-paragraph (2) for any child looked after—

    (a) in an appropriate children's home;

    (b) in a care home;

(c) as a patient in a hospital (within the meaning of the Care Standards Act 2000);

(d) in a residential family centre.

(2) The provision mentioned in sub-paragraph (1) is provision of day care made by—

(a) the department, authority or other person carrying on the establishment in question as part of the establishment's activities; or

(b) a person employed to work at that establishment and authorised to make that provision as part of the establishment's activities.

Exemption for occasional facilities

3.—(1) Where day care is provided on particular premises on less than six days in any year, that provision shall be disregarded for the purposes of Part XA if the person making it has notified the registration authority in writing before the first occasion on which the premises concerned are so used in that year.

(2) In sub-paragraph (1) "year" means the year beginning with the day (after the commencement of paragraph 5 of Schedule 9) on which the day care in question was or is first provided on the premises concerned and any subsequent year.

Disqualification for registration

4.—(1) Regulations may provide for a person to be disqualified for registration for child minding or providing day care.

(2) The regulations may, in particular, provide for a person to be disqualified where—

(a) he is included in the list kept under section 1 of the Protection of Children Act 1999; 1999 c. 14.

(b) he is included on the grounds mentioned in subsection (6ZA)(c) of section 218 of the Education Reform Act 1988 in the list kept for 1988 c. 40. the purposes of regulations made under subsection (6) of that section;

(c) an order of a prescribed kind has been made at any time with respect to him;

(d) an order of a prescribed kind has been made at any time with respect to any child who has been in his care;

(e) a requirement of a prescribed kind has been imposed at any time with respect to such a child, under or by virtue of any enactment;

(f) he has at any time been refused registration under Part X or Part XA or any prescribed enactment or had any such registration cancelled;

(g) he has been convicted of any offence of a prescribed kind, or has been placed on probation or discharged absolutely or conditionally for any such offence;

(h) he has at any time been disqualified from fostering a child privately;

(j) a prohibition has been imposed on him at any time under section 69, section 10 of the Foster Children (Scotland) Act 1984 or any 1984 c. 56. prescribed enactment;

(k) his rights and powers with respect to a child have at any time been vested in a prescribed authority under a prescribed enactment.

(3) Regulations may provide for a person who lives—

(a) in the same household as a person who is himself disqualified for registration for child minding or providing day care; or

(b) in a household at which any such person is employed,

to be disqualified for registration for child minding or providing day care.

(4) A person who is disqualified for registration for providing day care shall not provide day care, or be concerned in the management of, or have any financial interest in, any provision of day care.

(5) No person shall employ, in connection with the provision of day care, a person who is disqualified for registration for providing day care.

(6) In this paragraph "enactment" means any enactment having effect, at any time, in any part of the United Kingdom.

5.—(1) If any person—

(a) acts as a child minder at any time when he is disqualified for registration for child minding; or

(b) contravenes any of sub-paragraphs (3) to (5) of paragraph 4,

he shall be guilty of an offence.

(2) Where a person contravenes sub-paragraph (3) of paragraph 4, he shall not be guilty of an offence under this paragraph if he proves that he did not know, and had no reasonable grounds for believing, that the person in question was living or employed in the household.

(3) Where a person contravenes sub-paragraph (5) of paragraph 4, he shall not be guilty of an offence under this paragraph if he proves that he did not know, and had no reasonable grounds for believing, that the person whom he was employing was disqualified.

(4) A person guilty of an offence under this paragraph shall be liable on summary conviction to imprisonment for a term not exceeding six months, or to a fine not exceeding level 5 on the standard scale, or to both.

Certificates of registration

6.—(1) If an application for registration is granted, the registration authority shall give the applicant a certificate of registration.

(2) A certificate of registration shall give prescribed information about prescribed matters.

(3) Where, due to a change of circumstances, any part of the certificate requires to be amended, the registration authority shall issue an amended certificate.

(4) Where the registration authority is satisfied that the certificate has been lost or destroyed, the authority shall issue a copy, on payment by the registered person of any prescribed fee.

(5) For the purposes of Part XA, a person is—

(a) registered for providing child minding (in England or in Wales); or

(b) registered for providing day care on any premises,

if a certificate of registration to that effect is in force in respect of him.

Annual fees

7. Regulations may require registered persons to pay to the registration authority at prescribed times an annual fee of a prescribed amount.

Co-operation between authorities

8.—(1) Where it appears to the Chief Inspector that any local authority in England could, by taking any specified action, help in the exercise of any of his functions under Part XA, he may request the help of that authority specifying the action in question.

(2) Where it appears to the Assembly that any local authority in Wales could, by taking any specified action, help in the exercise of any of its functions under Part XA, the Assembly may request the help of that authority specifying the action in question.

(3) An authority whose help is so requested shall comply with the request if it is compatible with their own statutory or other duties and obligations and does not unduly prejudice the discharge of any of their functions."

SCHEDULE 4

Section 116.

MINOR AND CONSEQUENTIAL AMENDMENTS

National Assistance Act 1948 (c.29)

1.—(1) Section 26 of the National Assistance Act 1948 (provision of accommodation in premises maintained by voluntary organisations) shall be amended as follows.

(2) In subsection (1), for "(1B)" there shall be substituted "(1C)".

(3) For subsections (1A) and (1B) there shall be substituted—

"(1A) Arrangements must not be made by virtue of this section for the provision of accommodation together with nursing or personal care for persons such as are mentioned in section 3(2) of the Care Standards Act 2000 (care homes) unless—

    (a) the accommodation is to be provided, under the arrangements, in a care home (within the meaning of that Act) which is managed by the organisation or person in question; and

    (b) that organisation or person is registered under Part II of that Act in respect of the home."

(4) In subsection (1C), for the words from "no" to "person" there shall be substituted "no arrangements may be made by virtue of this section for the provision of accommodation together with nursing".

Mental Health Act 1959 (c.72)

2. In section 128 of the Mental Health Act 1959 (sexual intercourse with patients)—

    (a) in subsection (1), in paragraph (a), for "or mental nursing home" there shall be substituted ", independent hospital or care home" and in paragraph (b), for the words from "a residential" to the end there shall be substituted "a care home"; and

    (b) after subsection (5) there shall be inserted—

"(6) In this section "independent hospital" and "care home" have the same meanings as in the Care Standards Act 2000."

Children and Young Persons Act 1969 (c.54)

3. In section 23(12) of the Children and Young Persons Act 1969 (remands and committals to local authority accommodation)—

    (a) at the appropriate place, there shall be inserted—

        ""children's home" has the same meaning as in the Care Standards Act 2000;" and

    (b) in the definition of "secure accommodation"—

        (i) for "community home, a voluntary home or a registered children's home" there shall be substituted "children's home in respect of which a person is registered under Part II of the Care Standards Act 2000"; and

        (ii) at the end there shall be inserted "or the National Assembly for Wales".

Local Authority Social Services Act 1970 (c.42)

4. In Schedule 1 to the Local Authority Social Services Act 1970 (enactments conferring functions assigned to social services committee), in the entry relating to the 1989 Act, for "registered" there shall be substituted "private" and for "residential care, nursing or mental nursing homes or in independent schools" there shall be substituted "care homes, independent hospitals or schools".

Adoption Act 1976 (c.36)

5.—(1) The Adoption Act 1976 shall be amended as follows.

    (2) In section 1 (establishment of adoption service)—

    (a) in subsections (1), (3) and (4), for "approved adoption societies" and "approved adoption society", in each place where those words occur, there shall be substituted, respectively, "appropriate voluntary organisation" and "appropriate voluntary organisations"; and

    (b) after subsection (4) there shall be inserted—

        "(5) In this Act "appropriate voluntary organisation" means a voluntary organisation which is an adoption society in respect of which a person is registered under Part II of the Care Standards Act 2000."

(3) In section 2 (local authorities' social services), in paragraph (a), for "registered" there shall be substituted "private" and for "residential care, nursing or mental nursing homes or in independent schools" there shall be substituted "care homes, independent hospitals or schools".

(4) In section 4(3) of that Act (power of Secretary of State to make directions where approval of adoption society is withdrawn or expires), for the words from "Where" to "expires" there shall be substituted "Where, by virtue of the cancellation of the registration of any person under Part II of the Care Standards Act 2000, a body has ceased to be an appropriate voluntary organisation".

    (5) In section 8 (inactive or defunct adoption societies)—

    (a) in subsection (1), for the words from "an approved" to "expired" there shall be substituted "a body which is or has been an appropriate voluntary organisation"; and

    (b) for "society", in each place where it occurs, there shall be substituted "organisation".

    (6) In section 9 (regulation of adoption agencies)—

    (a) in subsection (2), for "an approved adoption society" there shall be substituted "an appropriate voluntary organisation";

    (b) after that subsection there shall be inserted—

"(2A) The power under subsection (2) includes in particular power to make in relation to an appropriate voluntary organisation any provision which regulations under section 22(2) or (7) of the Care Standards Act 2000 (regulation of establishments and agencies) may make in relation to a fostering agency (within the meaning of that Act).";

(c) after subsection (3) there shall be inserted—

"(3A) The power under subsection (3) includes in particular power to make in relation to the functions there mentioned any provision which regulations under section 48 of the Care Standards Act 2000 (regulation of the exercise of relevant fostering functions) may make in relation to relevant fostering functions (within the meaning of Part III of that Act)."; and

(d) in subsection (4), after "(2)" there shall be inserted "or (3)".

(7) In section 11 (restriction on arranging adoptions and placing of children)—

(a) in subsection (2), for "approved under section 3 of this Act" there shall be substituted "an appropriate voluntary organisation"; and

(b) in subsection (3)(a), for "which is not an adoption agency" there shall be substituted "which is not—

(i) a local authority; or

(ii) a voluntary adoption agency within the meaning of the Care Standards Act 2000 in respect of which he is registered;".

(8) In section 32 (meaning of "protected child")—

(a) in subsection (3)(a)(i), for "community home, voluntary home or registered children's home" there shall be substituted "children's home in respect of which a person is registered under Part II of the Care Standards Act 2000"; and

(b) in subsection (3A), for ""community home", "voluntary home", "registered children's home"" there shall be substituted ""children's home"".

(9) For section 51(3)(d)(i) there shall be substituted—

"(i) which is an appropriate voluntary organisation".

(10) In section 58A(1) (information concerning adoption), for "approved adoption society" there shall be substituted "appropriate voluntary organisation".

(11) In section 72(1) (interpretation), for the definition of "approved adoption society" there shall be substituted—

""appropriate voluntary organisation" has the meaning assigned by section 1(5);"

Adoption (Scotland) Act 1978 (c.28)

6. In section 11(2) of the Adoption (Scotland) Act 1978 (restriction on arranging adoptions and placing of children), for "approved as respects England and Wales under section 3 of the Adoption Act 1976" there shall be substituted "a person registered under Part II of the Care Standards Act 2000".

Magistrates' Court Act 1980 (c. 43)

7. In Schedule 6 to the Magistrates' Court Act 1980 (fees), in the entry relating to family proceedings, in the paragraph relating to the 1989 Act, for "Part X" there shall be substituted "Part XA".

Limitation Act 1980 (c.58)

8. In section 38 of the Limitation Act 1980 (interpretation)—

(a) in subsection (3), for the words from "within" to the end there is substituted "is incapable of managing and administering his property and affairs; and in this section "mental disorder" has the same meaning as in the Mental Health Act 1983"; and

(b) in subsection (4)(b), after "receiving treatment" there shall be inserted "for mental disorder" and for "or mental nursing home within the meaning of the Nursing Homes Act 1975" there shall be substituted "or independent hospital or care home within the meaning of the Care Standards Act 2000".

Mental Health Act 1983 (c.20)

9.—(1) The Mental Health Act 1983 shall be amended as follows.

(2) In sections 12(3), 23(3), 24(3), 46(1), 64(1), 119(2), 120(1) and (4), 131(1), 132(1), (2) and (4) and 133(1), for "mental nursing home" and "mental nursing homes" in each place where they occur, there shall be substituted, respectively, "registered establishment" and "registered establishments".

(3) In paragraph (b) of section 24(3) (visiting and examination of patients), for "Part II of the Registered Homes Act 1984" there shall be substituted "Part II of the Care Standards Act 2000".

(4) In section 34—

(a) in subsection (1), after the definition of "the nominated medical attendant" there shall be inserted—

""registered establishment" means an establishment—

(a) which would not, apart from subsection (2) below, be a hospital for the purposes of this Part; and

(b) in respect of which a person is registered under Part II of the Care Standards Act 2000 as an independent hospital in which treatment or nursing (or both) are provided for persons liable to be detained under this Act;" and

(b) in subsection (2), for the words from "a mental" to "1984" there shall be substituted "a registered establishment".

(5) In section 116(1) (welfare of certain hospital patients), for "or nursing home" there shall be substituted ", independent hospital or care home".

(6) In section 118(1) (code of practice)—

(a) for the first "and mental nursing homes" there shall be substituted ", independent hospitals and care homes"; and

(b) for the second "and mental nursing homes" there is substituted "and registered establishments".

(7) In section 121 (Mental Health Act Commission)—

(a) in subsection (4), for "and mental nursing homes" there shall be substituted ", independent hospitals and care homes"; and

(b) in subsection (5), in paragraphs (a) and (b), for "a mental nursing home" there shall be substituted "an independent hospital or a care home".

(8) In section 127(1) (ill-treatment of patients), for "or mental nursing home" there shall be substituted ", independent hospital or care home".

(9) In section 135(6) (warrant to search for and remove patients) for "a mental nursing home or residential home" there shall be substituted "an independent hospital or care home".

(10) In section 145(1) (interpretation)—

(a) after the definition of "approved social worker" there shall be inserted—

""care home" has the same meaning as in the Care Standards Act 2000";

(b) after the definition of "hospital order" and "guardianship order" there shall be inserted—

""independent hospital" has the same meaning as in the Care Standards Act 2000;"

(c) in the definition of "the managers", for paragraph (c) there shall be substituted—

"(c) in relation to a registered establishment, the person or persons registered in respect of the establishment;" and

(d) after the definition of "Primary Care Trust" there shall be inserted—

""registered establishment" has the meaning given in section 34 above;".

Public Health (Control of Disease) Act 1984 (c.22)

10. In section 7(4) of the Public Health (Control of Disease) Act 1984 (port health district and authority for Port of London), paragraphs (h) and (i) and the "and" following paragraph (i) shall be omitted.

Disabled Persons (Services, Consultation and Representation) Act 1986 (c.33)

11. In section 2(5)(d) of the Disabled Persons (Services, Consultation and Representation) Act 1986 (rights of authorised representatives of disabled persons), for "a residential care home within the meaning of Part I of the Registered Homes Act 1984" there shall be substituted "a care home within the meaning of the Care Standards Act 2000".

Adoption (Northern Ireland) Order 1987 (S.I. 1987/2203 (N.I.22))

12. In Article 11(2) of the Adoption (Northern Ireland) Order 1987 (restriction on arranging adoptions and placing children), for "approved as respects England and Wales under section 3 of the Adoption Act 1976 or as respects Scotland" there shall be substituted "in respect of which a person is registered under Part II of the Care Standards Act 2000 or which is approved as respects Scotland".

Income and Corporation Taxes Act 1988 (c.40)

13. In section 155A(6) of the Income and Corporation Taxes Act 1988 (care for children), after "section 71" there shall be inserted "or Part XA".

Children Act 1989 (c.41)

14.—(1) The 1989 Act shall be amended as follows.

(2) In section 19 (review of provision of day care, child minding etc.)—

(a) in subsection (1)(c), for "section 71(1)(b)" there shall be substituted "Part XA"; and

(b) in subsection (5), for the definition of "relevant establishment" there shall be substituted—

""relevant establishment" means—

(a) in relation to Scotland, any establishment which is mentioned in paragraphs 3 and 4 of Schedule 9 (establishments exempt from the registration requirements which apply in relation to the provision of day care in Scotland); and

(b) in relation to England and Wales, any establishment which is mentioned in paragraphs 1 and 2 of Schedule 9A (establishments exempt from the registration requirements which apply in relation to the provision of day care in England and Wales);".

(3) In section 23 (provision of accommodation and maintenance by local authority for children whom they are looking after)—

(a) in subsection (2), for paragraphs (b) to (e) there shall be substituted—

"(aa) maintaining him in an appropriate children's home;";

(b) after subsection (2) there shall be inserted—

"(2A) Where under subsection (2)(aa) a local authority maintains a child in a home provided, equipped and maintained by the Secretary of State under section 82(5), it shall do so on such terms as the Secretary of State may from time to time determine."; and

(c) after subsection (9) there shall be inserted—

"(10) In this Act—

"appropriate children's home" means a children's home in respect of which a person is registered under Part II of the Care Standards Act 2000; and

"children's home" has the same meaning as in that Act."

(4) In section 24 (advice and assistance for certain children), as it has effect before the commencement of section 4 of the Children (Leaving Care) Act 2000—

(a) in subsections (2)(c) and (12)(a), for "registered" there shall be substituted "private"; and

(b) in subsections (2)(d)(ii) and (12)(c), for "residential care home, nursing home or mental nursing home" there shall be substituted "care home or independent hospital".

(5) In section 24 (persons qualifying for advice and assistance) as it has effect after that commencement—

(a) in subsection (2)(c), for "registered" there shall be substituted "private"; and

(b) in subsection (2)(d)(ii), for "residential care home, nursing home or mental nursing home" there shall be substituted "care home or independent hospital".

(6) In section 24C(2) (information)—

(a) in paragraph (a), for "registered" there shall be substituted "private"; and

(b) in paragraph (c), for "residential care home, nursing home or mental nursing home" there shall be substituted "care home or independent hospital".

(7) In section 51(1) (refuges for children at risk), for "registered" there shall be substituted "private".

(8) In section 59 (provision of accommodation by voluntary organisations)—

(a) in subsection (1), for paragraphs (b) to (e) there shall be substituted—

"(aa) maintaining him in an appropriate children's home;"; and

(b) after that subsection there shall be inserted—

"(1A) Where under subsection (1)(aa) a local authority maintains a child in a home provided, equipped and maintained by the Secretary of State under section 82(5), it shall do so on such terms as the Secretary of State may from time to time determine."

(9) In section 60 (registration and regulation of voluntary homes)—

    (a) for the sidenote there shall be substituted "Voluntary homes."; and

    (b) for subsection (3) there shall be substituted—

      "(3) In this Act "voluntary home" means a children's home which is carried on by a voluntary organisation but does not include a community home."

(10) In section 62 (duties of local authorities in relation to children provided with accommodation by voluntary organisations)—

    (a) in subsection (6)(c), for "paragraph 7 of Schedule 5" there shall be substituted "section 22 of the Care Standards Act 2000"; and

    (b) after subsection (9) there shall be inserted—

      "(10) This section does not apply in relation to any voluntary organisation which is a school."

(11) In section 63 (children not to be cared for and accommodated in unregistered children's homes)—

    (a) for the sidenote there is substituted "Private children's homes etc.";

    (b) in subsection (11), after "to" there shall be inserted "private"; and

    (c) in subsection (12), after "treated" there shall be inserted ", for the purposes of this Act and the Care Standards Act 2000,".

(12) In section 64 (welfare of children in children's homes), in subsections (1) and (4), before "children's home" there shall be inserted "private".

(13) In section 65 (persons disqualified from carrying on, or being employed in, children's homes)—

    (a) in subsections (1) and (2), for "the responsible authority" and "their" there shall be substituted "the appropriate authority" and "its" respectively;

    (b) in subsection (3), for the words from "an" to "they" there shall be substituted "the appropriate authority refuses to give its consent under this section, it";

    (c) for subsection (3)(b) there shall be substituted—

      "(b) the applicant's right to appeal under section 65A against the refusal to the Tribunal established under section 9 of the Protection of Children Act 1999"; and

    (d) after subsection (5) there shall be inserted—

      "(6) In this section and section 65A "appropriate authority" means—

        (a) in relation to England, the National Care Standards Commission; and

        (b) in relation to Wales, the National Assembly for Wales."

1999 c. 14.

(14) After section 65 there is inserted—

"Appeal against refusal of authority to give consent under section 65.

65A.—(1) An appeal against a decision of an appropriate authority under section 65 shall lie to the Tribunal established under section 9 of the Protection of Children Act 1999.

    (2) On an appeal the Tribunal may confirm the authority's decision or direct it to give the consent in question."

(15) In section 66 (privately fostered children)—

    (a) in subsection (1)(a) after "accommodation" there shall be inserted "in their own home"; and

    (b) after subsection (4) there shall be inserted—

"(4A) The Secretary of State may by regulations make provision as to the circumstances in which a person who provides accommodation to a child is, or is not, to be treated as providing him with accommodation in the person's own home."

(16) In section 80 (inspection of children's homes etc by persons authorised by Secretary of State)—

(a) in subsections (1)(a) and (5)(c), before "children's" there shall be inserted "private";

(b) in subsection (1)(i), after "71(1)(b)" there shall be added "or with respect to which a person is registered for providing day care under Part XA";

(c) for subsection (1)(j) there shall be substituted—

"(j) care home or independent hospital used to accommodate children;" and

(d) in subsection (5), after paragraph (h) there shall be inserted—

"(hh) person who is the occupier of any premises—

(i) in which any person required to be registered for child minding under Part XA acts as a child minder (within the meaning of that Part); or

(ii) with respect to which a person is required to be registered under that Part for providing day care;".

(17) In section 81(1) (inquiries)—

(a) in paragraph (d), after "a" there shall be inserted "private"; and

(b) in paragraph (e), for "a residential care home, nursing home or mental nursing home" there shall be substituted "a care home or independent hospital".

(18) In section 82(6) (financial support by Secretary of State), in the definition of "child care training", for "residential care home, nursing home or mental nursing home" there shall be substituted "care home or independent hospital".

(19) In section 83 (research and returns of information), in subsections (1)(c), (2)(c) and (3)(a)(ii), for "residential care home, nursing home or mental nursing home" there shall be substituted "care home or independent hospital".

(20) In section 86—

(a) for the sidenote there shall be substituted "Children accommodated in care homes or independent hospitals."; and

(b) in subsections (1) and (5), for "residential care home, nursing home or mental nursing home" there shall be substituted "care home or independent hospital".

(21) For the sidenote to section 87 (welfare of children accommodated in independent schools) there shall be substituted "Welfare of children in boarding schools and colleges.".

(22) In section 102(6)(a) (power of constable to assist in exercise of certain powers to search for children or inspect premises), after "76," there shall be inserted "79U,".

(23) In section 105 (interpretation)—

(a) in subsection (1)—

(i) after the definition of "adoption agency" there shall be inserted—

""appropriate children's home" has the meaning given by section 23;"

(ii) after the definition of "bank holiday" there shall be inserted—

""care home" has the same meaning as in the Care Standards Act 2000;"

(iii) for the definition of "children's home" there shall be substituted—

""children's home" has the meaning given by section 23;"

(iv) in the definition of "day care", after "care"" there shall be inserted "(except in Part XA)";

(v) in the definition of "hospital", after "hospital" there shall be inserted "(except in Schedule 9A)";

(vi) after the definition of "income-based jobseeker's allowance" there shall be inserted—

""independent hospital" has the same meaning as in the Care Standards Act 2000;" and

(vii) after the definition of "prescribed" there shall be inserted—

""private children's home" means a children's home in respect of which a person is registered under Part II of the Care Standards Act 2000 which is not a community home or a voluntary home;"; and

(b) after subsection (5) there shall be inserted—

"(5A) References in this Act to a child minder shall be construed—

(a) in relation to Scotland, in accordance with section 71;

(b) in relation to England and Wales, in accordance with section 79A.".

(24) In Schedule 3 (supervision orders), in paragraphs 4(2)(c)(ii) and 5(2)(c), for "or mental nursing home" there shall be substituted ", independent hospital or care home".

(25) In Schedule 6 (registered children's homes)—

(a) in the heading, for "Registered Children's Homes" there shall be substituted "Private Children's Homes"; and

(b) in paragraph 10(1)(a), for "registered" there shall be substituted "private".

(26) In paragraph 5(1) of Schedule 7 (foster parents: limit on number of foster children), after "treated" there shall be inserted ", for the purposes of this Act and the Care Standards Act 2000".

(27) In Schedule 8 (privately fostered children)—

(a) in paragraph 2, sub-paragraph (1)(b) shall cease to have effect, and in sub-paragraph (2), for "(1)(b)" there shall be substituted "(1)(c)"; and

(b) in paragraph 9(1), for "2(1)(d)" there shall be substituted "2(1)(c) and (d)", and at the end there shall be inserted—

"But this sub-paragraph does not apply to a school which is an appropriate children's home.".

(28) For paragraph 2(1)(f) of Schedule 8 (privately fostered children) there shall be substituted—

"(f) in any care home or independent hospital;".

(29) In paragraph 4(1) of Schedule 9 (child minding and day care for young children)—

(a) for paragraphs (a) to (c) there shall be substituted—

"(aa) an appropriate children's home;" and

(b) for paragraph (d) there shall be substituted—

"(d) a care home;".

National Health Service and Community Care Act 1990 (c.19)

15. In section 48(1) of the National Health Service and Community Care Act 1990 (inspection of premises used for the provision of community care), for "the Registered Homes Act 1984" there shall be substituted "Part II of the Care Standards Act 2000".

Criminal Procedure (Insanity and Unfitness to Plead) Act 1991 (c.25)

16. In paragraph 4(2)(a) of Schedule 2 to the Criminal Procedure (Insanity and Unfitness to Plead) Act 1991 (supervision and treatment orders), for "hospital or mental nursing home" there shall be substituted "independent hospital or care home within the meaning of the Care Standards Act 2000 or in a hospital".

Criminal Justice Act 1991 (c.53)

17. In section 61(2) of the Criminal Justice Act 1991 (provision by local authorities of secure accommodation), for the words from "voluntary" to the end there shall be substituted "persons carrying on an appropriate children's home for the provision or use by them of such accommodation".

Water Industry Act 1991 (c.56)

18. In Schedule 4A to the Water Industry Act 1991 (premises that are not to be disconnected for non-payment of charges), for paragraphs 8 and 9 there shall be substituted—

　　"8.—(1) A care home or independent hospital.

　　(2) In this paragraph—

　　　"care home" means—

　　　　　(a) a care home within the meaning of the Care Standards Act 2000;

　　　　　(b) a building or part of a building in which residential accommodation is provided under section 21 of the National Assistance Act 1948;

　　　"independent hospital" means an independent hospital within the meaning of the Care Standards Act 2000.

　　　9. A children's home within the meaning of the Care Standards Act 2000."

19. In Schedule 4A to the Water Industry Act 1991 (premises that are not to be disconnected for non-payment of charges), in paragraph 12 for "section 71(1)(b)" there shall be substituted "Part XA".

Local Government Finance Act 1992 (c.14)

20. In paragraph 7 of Schedule 1 to the Local Government Finance Act 1992 (persons disregarded for purposes of discount)—

　　(a) in sub-paragraph (1)(a), for "residential care home, nursing home, mental nursing home" there shall be substituted "care home, independent hospital";

　　(b) in sub-paragraph (1)(b), after "home" there shall be inserted ", hospital";

　　(c) for sub-paragraph (2), there shall be substituted—

　　"(2) In this paragraph—

　　　"care home" means—

　　　　　(a) a care home within the meaning of the Care Standards Act 2000; or

(b) a building or part of a building in which residential accommodation is provided under section 21 of the National Assistance Act 1948;

"hostel" means anything which falls within any definition of hostel for the time being prescribed by order made by the Secretary of State under this sub-paragraph;

"independent hospital" has the same meaning as in the Care Standards Act 2000." and

(d) in sub-paragraph (3), for ""mental nursing home", "nursing home" or "residential care home"" there shall be substituted ""care home" or "independent hospital"".

Tribunals and Inquiries Act 1992 (c.53)

21. In Schedule 1 to the Tribunals and Inquiries Act 1992 (tribunals under supervision of Council), paragraph 36A (inserted by paragraph 8 of the Schedule to the Protection of Children Act 1999) is renumbered as paragraph 36B and, in the first column of that paragraph, after "Protection of children" there shall be inserted "and vulnerable adults, and care standards".

Criminal Justice and Public Order Act 1994 (c.33)

22. In section 2 of the Criminal Justice and Public Order Act 1994 (secure training orders: supplementary provisions as to detention)—

(a) in subsection (5), for "registered children's home" there shall be substituted "private children's home"; and

(b) in subsection (8), for "registered children's home" there shall be substituted "private children's home".

Children (Scotland) Act 1995 (c.36)

23. In section 93 of the Children (Scotland) Act 1995 (interpretation of Part II)—

(a) in paragraph (b) of the definition of "residential establishment", for "registered" there shall be substituted "private"; and

(b) in the definition of "secure accommodation", for "paragraph 4(2)(i) of Schedule 4 to the Children Act 1989" there shall be substituted "section 22(8)(a) of the Care Standards Act 2000".

Education Act 1996 (c.56)

24.—(1) The Education Act 1996 shall be amended as follows.

(2) In section 467(2) (provision of information about registered and provisionally registered schools), for "Children Act 1989" there shall be substituted "Care Standards Act 2000".

(3) In section 469(4) (notice of complaint by Secretary of State), after "school is" there shall be inserted "unsuitable to work with children or is for any other reason".

(4) In section 471(2)(a) (determination of complaint by Secretary of State), after "school is" there shall be inserted "unsuitable to work with children or is for any other reason".

Police Act 1997 (c.50)

25.—(1) In section 113(3A) of the Police Act 1997 (criminal record certificates), for "suitability for" there shall be substituted "suitability to be employed, supplied to work, found work or given work in".

(2) In section 115 of that Act (enhanced criminal record certificates)—

(a) in subsection (5)(e), for "or" there shall be substituted "registration for child minding or providing day care under Part XA of that Act or registration under"; and

(b) in subsection (6A), for "suitability for" there shall be substituted "suitability to be employed, supplied to work, found work or given work in".

Protection of Children Act 1999 (c.14)

26.—(1) The Protection of Children Act 1999 shall be amended as follows.

(2) In section 2 (inclusion in list on reference to Secretary of State)—

(a) in subsection (2)(b), for "or retired", in each place where those words occur, there shall be substituted ", retired or made redundant"; and

(b) in subsection (8)(a), for "or retiring" there shall be substituted ", retiring or being made redundant" and for "or retired" there shall be substituted ", retired or been made redundant".

(2) In section 7 (effect of inclusion in the lists kept under section 1 of the 1999 Act and section 218(6) of the Education Reform Act 1988)—

1988 c. 40.

(a) after subsection (1) there shall be inserted—

"(1A) Where a child care organisation discovers that an individual employed by it in a child care position is included in any of the lists mentioned in subsection (1) above, it shall cease to employ him in a child care position.

For the purposes of this subsection an individual is not employed in a child care position if he has been suspended or provisionally transferred to a position which is not a child care position."; and

(b) in subsection (2), after "employment agency" there shall be inserted "or an employment business".

(3) In section 9 (the Tribunal)—

(a) in subsection (2), for the words from "on an appeal" to the end there shall be substituted—

"(a) on an appeal or determination under section 4 above;

(b) on an appeal under regulations made under section 6 above;

1989 c. 41.

(c) on an appeal under section 65A of the Children Act 1989 or under, or by virtue of, Part XA of that Act; or

(d) on an appeal or determination under section 21, 68, 86, 87 or 88 of the Care Standards Act 2000;"; and

(b) after subsection (3), there shall be inserted—

"(3A) The regulations may also include provision for enabling the Tribunal to make investigations for the purposes of a determination under section 87 or 88 of the Care Standards Act 2000; and the provision that may be made by virtue of subsection (3)(j) and (k) above includes provision in relation to such investigations.

(3B) Regulations under this section may make different provision for different cases or classes of case.

(3C) Before making in regulations under this section provision such as is mentioned in subsection (2)(c) or (d) above, the Secretary of State shall consult the National Assembly for Wales."

(4) In section 12 (interpretation)—

(a) in subsection (1)—

(i) in the definition of "employment agency", for "has the same meaning" there shall be substituted "and "employment business" have the same meanings"; and

(ii) after the definition of "harm" there shall be inserted—

""local authority" has the same meaning as in the Children Act 1989;"; and

(b) after subsection (3) there shall be inserted—

"(3A) For the purposes of this Act, an individual is made redundant if—

(a) he is dismissed; and

(b) for the purposes of the Employment Rights Act 1996 the dismissal is by reason of redundancy."

Adoption (Intercountry Aspects) Act 1999 (c.18)

27. In section 2 of the Adoption (Intercountry Aspects) Act 1999 (central authorities and accredited bodies)—

(a) after subsection (2) there shall be inserted—

"(2A) A voluntary adoption agency in respect of which a person is registered under Part II of the Care Standards Act 2000 is an accredited body for the purposes of the Convention if, in accordance with the conditions of the registration, the agency may provide facilities in respect of Convention adoptions and adoptions effected by Convention adoption orders."; and

(b) for subsection (5) there shall be substituted—

"(5) In this section in its application to England and Wales, "voluntary adoption agency" has the same meaning as in the Care Standards Act 2000; and expressions which are also used in the Adoption Act 1976 ("the 1976 Act") have the same meanings as in that Act."

1976 c. 36.

Powers of Criminal Courts (Sentencing) Act 2000 (c.6)

28.—(1) The Powers of Criminal Courts (Sentencing) Act 2000 shall be amended as follows.

(2) In paragraph 5(3)(a) of Schedule 2 (additional requirements which may be included in probation orders), for "a hospital or mental nursing home" there shall be substituted "an independent hospital or care home within the meaning of the Care Standards Act 2000 or a hospital".

(3) In paragraph 6(2)(a) of Schedule 6 (requirements which may be included in supervision orders), for "a hospital or mental nursing home" there shall be substituted "an independent hospital or care home within the meaning of the Care Standards Act 2000 or a hospital".

Amendments of local Acts

29.—(1) Section 16 of the Greater London Council (General Powers) Act 1981 (exemption from provisions of Part IV of the Act of certain premises) shall be amended as follows.

1981 c. xvii.

(2) For paragraph (g) there shall be substituted—

"(g) used as a care home, or an independent hospital, within the meaning of the Care Standards Act 2000;"

(3) For paragraphs (gg) and (h) there shall be substituted—

"(gg) used as a children's home within the meaning of the Care Standards Act 2000 which is a home in respect of which a person is registered under Part II of that Act;"

(4) Paragraph (j) shall be omitted.

1984 c. xxvii.   30.—(1) Section 10(2) of the Greater London Council (General Powers) Act 1984 (exemption from provisions of Part IV of the Act of certain premises) shall be amended as follows.

(2) For paragraph (c) there shall be substituted—

"(c) used as a care home, or an independent hospital, within the meaning of the Care Standards Act 2000;"

(3) For paragraph (d) there shall be substituted—

"(d) used as a children's home within the meaning of the Care Standards Act 2000 which is a home in respect of which a person is registered under Part II of that Act;"

(4) Paragraphs (f) and (l) shall be omitted.

Section 117(1).   SCHEDULE 5

TRANSITIONAL PROVISIONS AND SAVINGS

Fostering agencies

1. The appropriate Minister may by regulations provide that, if prescribed requirements are satisfied, section 11 shall apply, during the prescribed period, to a person running a fostering agency who has made an application for registration under section 12(1) as if that person were unconditionally registered under Part II of this Act.

Voluntary adoption agencies

2.—(1) Where an approval granted to a body, before the commencement of section 13, under section 3 of the Adoption Act 1976 (approval of adoption societies) is operative at that commencement, Part II of this Act shall, if prescribed requirements are satisfied, have effect after that commencement as if any person carrying on or managing the body were registered under that Part in respect of it, either—

1976 c. 36.

(a) unconditionally; or

(b) subject to such conditions as may be prescribed.

(2) Any application made before the commencement of section 12 for approval under section 3 of the Adoption Act 1976 shall be treated after that commencement as an application made under section 12(1) to the registration authority for registration under Part II of this Act.

(3) The appropriate Minister may by order make such further transitional provision in relation to the repeal by this Act of provisions of the Adoption Act 1976 as he considers appropriate.

Children's Commissioner for Wales

3.—(1) The Part of this Act which relates to the Children's Commissioner for Wales has effect, in relation to times before the commencement of any other relevant provision of this Act, as if references—

(a) to regulated children's services in Wales; and

(b) to the provider of such services,

were or included references to services which would be regulated children's services in Wales, or (as the case may be) to the person who would be the provider, if that provision were in force.

(2) Sub-paragraph (1) has effect subject to any provision made under sections 118 or 119.

SCHEDULE 6

REPEALS

Section 117(2).

Chapter	Short title	Extent of repeal
1948 c. 29.	National Assistance Act 1948.	Section 26(1E).
1957 c. 16.	Nurses Agencies Act 1957.	The whole Act.
1958 c. 51.	Public Records Act 1958.	In Schedule 1, in the Table at the end of paragraph 3, in Part II, the entry relating to the Care Council for Wales.
1963 c. 33.	London Government Act 1963.	Section 40(4)(i).
1970 c. 42.	Local Authority Social Services Act 1970.	In Schedule 1, in the entry relating to the Mental Health Act 1959, the words "and the Registered Homes Act 1984 so far as its provisions relate to mental nursing homes", and the entry relating to the Registered Homes Act 1984.
1970 c. 44.	Chronically Sick and Disabled Persons Act 1970.	Section 18.
1972 c. 70.	Local Government Act 1972.	In Schedule 29, paragraph 30.
1973 c. 35.	Employment Agencies Act 1973.	In section 13(7), paragraphs (b) and (c) and the proviso.
1976 c. 36.	Adoption Act 1976.	Section 3. Section 4(1) and (2). In section 4(3), the word "concerned". Section 5. Section 9(1).
1979 c. 36.	Nurses, Midwives and Health Visitors Act 1979.	In Schedule 7, paragraphs 8, 9 and 10.
1981 c. xvii.	Greater London Council (General Powers) Act 1981.	Section 16(j).

Chapter	Short title	Extent of repeal
1983 c. 20.	Mental Health Act 1983.	In section 145(1), the definition of "mental nursing home".
1983 c. 41.	Health and Social Services and Social Security Adjudications Act 1983.	In Schedule 2, paragraph 29.
1984 c. 22.	Public Health (Control of Disease) Act 1984.	In section 7(4), paragraphs (h) and (i) and the "and" following paragraph (i).
1984 c. 23.	Registered Homes Act 1984.	The whole Act.
1984 c. xxvii.	Greater London Council (General Powers) Act 1984.	Section 10(2)(f) and (l).
1989 c. 41.	Children Act 1989.	Section 54. In section 58(1), the word "54(2)". In section 60, subsections (1) and (2), and in subsection (3)(a), the words "(other than a small home)". Section 63(1) to (10). In section 80(4), the word "or" before paragraph (d). In section 104(1), the word "54(2)". In section 105(1), the definitions of "child minder", "mental nursing home", "nursing home", "registered children's home" and "residential care home". In Schedule 4, in paragraph 4, sub-paragraphs (1)(b) and (c), (2) and (3). In Schedule 5, paragraphs 1 to 6, in paragraph 7, sub-paragraphs (1)(b) and (c) and (2) to (4), and paragraph 8. In Schedule 6, paragraphs 1 to 9 and in paragraph 10, sub-paragraphs (1)(b) and (c), (2)(a) to (k), (3) and (4). In Schedule 8, paragraph 2(1)(b) and in paragraph 9(1), the words "which is not maintained by a local education authority". In Schedule 13, paragraph 49, in paragraph 73, sub-paragraphs (2) and (3) and in paragraph 74, sub-paragraphs (2) and (4).

Chapter	Short title	Extent of repeal
1990 c. 19.	National Health Service and Community Care Act 1990.	In Schedule 9, paragraph 27.
1991 c. 20.	Registered Homes (Amendment) Act 1991.	The whole Act.
1992 c. 53.	Tribunals and Inquiries Act 1992.	In Schedule 1, the entry relating to the Registered Homes Tribunals constituted under Part III of the Registered Homes Act 1984.
1993 c. 8.	Judicial Pensions and Retirement Act 1993.	In Schedule 5, the entry relating to a Chairman of a Registered Homes Tribunal constituted under the Registered Homes Act 1984. In Schedule 6, paragraph 55. In Schedule 7, paragraph 5(5)(xxxi).
1994 c. 19.	Local Government (Wales) Act 1994.	In Schedule 9, paragraph 5.
1996 c. 23.	Arbitration Act 1996.	In Schedule 3, paragraph 41.
1996 c. 56.	Education Act 1996.	In Schedule 37, paragraphs 58, 86, 88 and 89.
1997 c. 24.	Nurses, Midwives and Health Visitors Act 1997.	In Schedule 4, paragraph 3.
1999 c. 14.	Protection of Children Act 1999.	In section 2(9), the words "or an agency for the supply of nurses". In section 7(2), the words "or an agency for the supply of nurses". Section 10. In section 12(1), the definition of "agency for the supply of nurses". Section 13(3) and (4).
1999 c. 18.	Adoption (Intercountry Aspects) Act 1999.	Section 10.

Printed in the UK by The Stationery Office Limited
under the authority and superintendence of Carol Tullo, Controller of
Her Majesty's Stationery Office and Queen's Printer of Acts of Parliament

Dd 758413   11/2000   19585

1st Impression July 2000
2nd Impression November 2000